50¢

82

The Poems of Sextus Propertius

The Poems of
Sextus Propertius

Translated with an Introduction by

J. P. McCULLOCH

University of California Press, Berkeley, Los Angeles, London

University of California Press
Berkeley and Los Angeles, California
University of California Press, Ltd.
London, England
Copyright © 1972 by:
The Regents of the University of California
First Paperback Edition, 1974
ISBN: 0-520-02774-4
Library of Congress Catalog Card Number: 78-115490
Printed in the United States of America

Contents

Introduction

THE ALERT reader will quickly discover that in these poems Propertius did not write his autobiography; they contain too many opacities and contradictions to make sense as a personal history of the poet, at least as the kind of personal history that would satisfy the careful scholar. Unfortunately, facts about Propertius from other sources are scanty. There are, however, fragmentary bits of information found in the poems and elsewhere which everyone agrees are more likely to be true than otherwise.

Propertius was born about 50 B.C., probably in Assisi, although there is some learned contention on this point. He was young when his father died, and part of the family estate—it was an equestrian family—was confiscated in the land seizures of 40 B.C. Although he was obviously well educated, Propertius admits that he had no inclination to take up law, the usual career of a young man of his class and education. He may, however, have traveled abroad, thus enjoying a customary preoccupation of his peers.

For several years Propertius carried on an affair with "Cynthia" (whose real name was probably Hostia); an educated freedwoman and a courtesan, she possessed considerable ability. She had light hair and dark eyes, and was sexually attractive. The affair was not a harmonious one, and, as revealed by the final poem in Book III, Propertius and Cynthia parted in bitterness. In a later poem (IV.7) Propertius is either suggesting that a reconciliation took place before Cynthia died (not long after the separation), or is simply recalling earlier and happier memories once his love was dead. He may have married and fathered children after Cynthia died. He died fairly young, probably about the age of forty.

These details are, for the most part, unimportant, for the real Propertius lives in his works. Although Propertius did not write for the historian, the reader of his poems, even in the poorest translation, encounters brilliantly illuminated bits of a man's life and thoughts. Thus the poems, with allowances made for poetic license, convey a good deal of information about Propertius. What is revealed is his mind, a mind of considerable genius and peculiarity. He is a romantic; and, as Professor J. P. Sullivan has pointed out (in "Cynthia Prima Fuit: A Causerie," *Arion*, I [Autumn, 1962]), he may well have been an early example of a Freudian type:

> Freud describes this character-type, which is not neurotic but found among ordinary healthy people and even among people of exceptional qualities, in the following way. Such men require certain conditions before they fall in love—"the need of an injured party," husband, betrothed, or lover; it must be "love of a harlot," although this element may depend on anything from the faintest breath of scandal attaching to a flirtatious wife up to the open sexual immorality of a prostitute or a *grande amoureuse*. And this last, which suggests the possibility of her being unfaithful to him, is connected to the jealousy necessary for such lovers.

In my opinion Sullivan's view of this aspect of the poet's personality is correct, but the reader may judge for himself. Certainly it is true that Propertius inclined toward an involvement with women which was adventurous even by Roman standards. The first poem in Book I clearly reveals his feelings about marriageable women, and II.7 expresses his views on the prospect of respectable matrimony. Propertius is really "married" to Cynthia, and he would have it no other way. When rejected by his beloved courtesan, he resorts to boys and to a less fortunate class of prostitutes, but always he hopes for a reconciliation with his real love. When he declares he will have no more to do with bawds, it is merely *accismus*, a convention of the times.

The love poems and those dealing with death have the ring of strong conviction. Horace never looks at death in the alarmed and unphilosophical way Propertius does, for death in Propertius is a much more personal and fearful thing than in the customary rhetoric of Augustan Rome. Propertius dreads death; he lives with it in fascination. His obsession with death, second only to his obsession with Cynthia, is neither stoic nor in any way cowardly. "Romantic" is the word that again comes to mind:

> I am not afraid now
>   of the shadowy afterlife,
>   nor do I pine away
>   thinking of fate's due,
>   the ultimate bonefire;
> But I do fear
>   that your love's strength
>   will not survive until my funeral . . .

Propertius writes of more than love and death, though these concerns are at the center of his great poems. Pastoral fantasies, travelogues, friendships, and myths find a place; and above all, there is Rome. Unlike his contemporaries Horace and Tibullus, he was strictly a city poet. Rome, the imperial city, comes alive in the pages of Propertius. It is rather an odd place, as a quick glance at IV.8 will show.

Since Propertius did not admire everything about imperial Rome, he infused his ceremonial and patriotic poems with an irony difficult to mistake. Mistake, though, was the rule until Ezra Pound seized upon Propertius and actually read the Latin. Pound has been unjustly faulted for his lack of scholarship, but several generations of learned men before him might more justly be condemned for want of sensibility. If the critics who damned Pound's interpretation of Propertius would read a modern poet the way they read Propertius, they would universally be thought dense. Propertius was at least as great and subtle a poet as, say, T. S. Eliot. Propertian scholarship before Pound looked more at the word and the phrase than at the whole poem or the corpus of poems. Can any man now believe that Propertius meant to honor Augustus in IV.6, or to glorify conquest in III.4? Could not some of the dreadful poems in Book IV be mock-heroic? If so, they would be at least comprehensible, though scarcely less dreadful. Let those who wish go to the text, but in doing so they should keep in mind that the poet who wrote IV.10 also wrote IV.11. The best and most obviously sincere poems in Book IV were written for women.

Aside from the hypothesis of the poet's anti-imperialism (the alternative seems to me to be the poet's mental decay), it is undeniable that Propertius was an unwilling conscript as a court poet:

> But Callimachus has a narrow chest,
>   cannot rumble with enough majesty
>   for the godly songs,
> Nor can my diaphragm sustain

the rough verses of Caesar's Trojan lineage.

. . . .

To each his own tune . . .

Maecenas has been spoken of as Augustus' "minister of propaganda," and it is certain that he pressured Propertius, as he would have pressured any poet of merit in that period, to write patriotic, official verse. Propertius acquiesced, with the enthusiasm to be expected of a sly and beleaguered love poet, but I do not see that he ever bit the hand of his patron. Propertius, either prudently or as a friend of Maecenas, kept his sarcasm low-keyed and directed it at other targets. The poems that insist upon Maecenas' peaceable virtues may have their share of irony, but I doubt it. Propertius was certainly more cautious than Ovid, undoubtedly because his disagreements with the Emperor were based on principle, not on style and temperament.

Propertius was not the first Latin elegist. Catullus occasionally used the elegiac meter, and Gallus, whose poems are lost, may have made it the conventional medium for subjective love poems. Quintilian preferred the elegiac verse of Tibullus to that of Propertius, but fairly pointed out that some readers liked Propertius better. Propertius was writing in the middle of a tradition; yet one has to keep in mind the differences between poets in that tradition, most of all between Propertius and Tibullus and Ovid. Tibullus' pastoral settings and limpid style are another world; Ovid learned and borrowed much from Propertius, but a gulf separates them because Ovid did not take women seriously. This disparity of temper is far more important than any divergence in technique. There is no frivolity—and no contempt—in Propertius' attitude toward women.

The elegiac meter is Greek. The early Greek elegy was

[5]

occasionally a metric for love poetry, but the Alexandrian tradition in which Propertius took so much trouble to place himself was not a tradition of the subjective love poem, or scarcely of the love poem at all. That a poet should be a learned man, Propertius took from Callimachus—and also the idea that "a fat book is a lot of crap." The love elegy is Latin, and Propertius is its greatest master.

Anyone who would translate Propertius must justify doing so in the light of Pound's *Homage to Sextus Propertius*, itself a great English poem. Pound responded to the foolish criticism of his poem by denying, with his usual vehemence, that it was meant to be a translation of Propertius. Despite Pound's denial, however, *Homage to Sextus Propertius* is, by customary standards, a translation, a masterly and extraordinary translation. There is scarcely anything in it which does not have a clear origin in the Latin. What gives a translator the right to try again is not any defect in Pound's poem, but rather the purpose of the poet. Pound translated selectively and to his own ends, and he left a lot of excellent poetry in the original. Moreover, the structure of Propertius' poetry is unlike that of Pound's in *Homage*. The looseness and the digressiveness of the Latin, though usually not deemed virtues, in my opinion give the poems a rich and suggestive texture which is worth trying to reproduce in English. Pound strung his hard and brilliant fragments together in a way that produced a different quality, a richness and suggestiveness of another kind. It is important to remember that Pound never intended to translate into English a large portion of Propertius' Latin poetry.

My translation is not always faithful to the Latin text. I have added a few lines of my own, usually transitional, and have deleted perhaps a score of lines from the original. The omissions stem from the best of all reasons: I could not, in the context in which I found the lines, translate them into

English. In three or four instances mistakes I inadvertently made in translating seemed so much better than the correct renditions that I have kept them. Occasionally I have moved lines from one place to another. Those who object to the liberties I have taken should seek out more literal translations or, if they enjoy reading Latin poetry, should go to the original text of Propertius.

In arrangement, I have for the most part followed the Loeb edition. I have accepted the customary division of Propertius into four books, although I question the validity of arguments against division into five books. Yet to disturb tradition and mark out a new path would be to inconvenience the reader. I have departed from the Loeb text in using Arabic instead of Roman numerals for individual poems, and also in occasionally combining several poems under one numeral heading. For example, I have rendered as one poem, II.18, the three poems numbered II.xviii, II.xviiiA, and II.xviiiB in Loeb.

I am grateful to the National Translation Center for its generous grant and to the editors of *Arion* and *Delos*, who printed several of my translations of these poems, for their encouraging interest. The advice and criticism of James Hynd were most helpful, and without the assistance of Kay and Odin Toness and Sara Clark I would never have finished this translation.

The Poems of Sextus Propertius

BOOK I

1

The flame first arose
    with the gleam in her eye,
& I bent my head then,
    lowered a proud glance
    at Eros' insistence,
       & thus I learned.
& a hard passion taught me
    to abhor virgin girls,
    taught me also
      to live without benefit of discretion.
For a year now, this madness, unfaltering
  though the gods float hostile above me.
Yet he fled no hard labor,
    who captured Atalanta
    fleet-foot & flint-hearted though she was.
He wavered through Parthenian caverns,
    faced lank-haired beasts in the forests,
    defended her against the centaur Hylaeus
    & got his head cracked for it,
  & lay wounded on the cliffs,
but Milanion's devotion broke and won
    swift-footed loveliness.
Thus effort & devoted prayer
    may do some good, occasionally,
  but for me,
    Aphrodite is languid,

forgets her art
       & craft & former ways.
You magicians who delude with moon rays
    and consecrate witchwork at the magic cauldron,
  come change the way Cynthia's heart beats against me,
    turn her lips paler [1] than my own;
Then only will I credit your claim
      to dominion over river & star
  with Medea's arcane song.
And my friends, you are much too late,
      who would lift me up—
but still, seek some way
    to take this coal from my heart.
I will undergo iron and fire with fortitude,
    but release this voice
    broken by desire,
that I may speak out against her.
Arrange my passage past all borders
    to the ocean's uttermost rim,
  where no woman may perceive the way.
Whosoever shares a secure and lasting love,
    stay here at home, if the gods
    hear your lifted invocation.
For me passion's taste is bitter in the night;
    solitary love never fails.
& I warn you, avoid the evil.
    Let each man cleave
    to a faithful woman, when
  and if decorous love has found its place.
& I promise you this,
    if you don't attend my words
      you will remember them in affliction.

[1] In Latin poetry, pale lips and cheeks customarily signified a dismayed lover.

2

Why go forth in the streets
    with elegant coiffure, my love,
        moving in subtle curves of Coan [2] vestment,
Orontean myrrh in your hair,
        advertising peregrine adornments?
Why cover native grace
        with commercial refinement,
    when your beauty is radiant on undecorated limbs?
No herbs can improve
        so beautiful a figure,
    & naked Eros loves no contrived beauty.
Consider what fine colors
        strike from the rude earth;
    wild ivy is the best ivy,
    & the most splendid arbutus
            surges from backwoods caves,
    and wild streams glitter
            in untutored streambeds.
Our Italic shores persuade us
        with pebbles, their native jewels,
    and the birds sing without any instruction.

It was not Phoebe's cosmetics
        that set a fire under Castor,
    nor was Pollux kindled with such refinements;
No jewelry raised ancient discord
        between Idas and inflamed Apollo,
    nor was Hippodamia carried off in a strange chariot

[2] The island of Cos plays a large role in Propertius' poems. Its silks
and wines were symbolic of other riches, such as Philetas and his verse
and, by extension, elegiac verse in general, particularly that of Pro-
pertius.

      due to the dazzle
of unnatural radiance.
These worthy beauties depended on no gemstones,
        and the glow of their faces
    was of surpassing excellence,
        better than Apelles' paintings,
and they burned for no multitude of lovers,
        and virtue was sufficient adornment to beauty.

I fear for good reason. . . .
        I would not be thought less of
            than those others. . . .
To be able to please one man
            is adornment enough
    when Phoebus presents you with song
    & Calliope grants you her Aonian lyre
    & your words please my ear uniquely;
All these virtues please Minerva,
        and Aphrodite also;
& by their grace
            you will always be to me
            most charming;
For me you need no extravagances.

3

Like Ariadne languid on desert beach,
   Theseus' keel laid into the sea
      & departing,
Or like Andromeda sleeping close by the flint
   she was strung to so lately,
Or a maenad lying limp
   from her dance
      among riverine herbs;
So Cynthia's breast heaved in supple rest
   head cradled loosely in her hands
      when I came in drunk, stumbling
        with wine fumes,
  the glass run out
    & the flame trembling in the slave boy's hands.
But with desire unquenched
   I undertook soft approach,
     bent onto the couch
      burning with two fires;
  lewd Liber laid hold of me,
        and then Eros, one hard as the other.
Lightly I tried to embrace
   her sleeping form,
     kissed her covetously,
Yet I feared to wake
     my brawl-proven Cynthia,
       fearing her claws,
but like Argus gazed raptly,
   and I put my wreath in your hair,
   and as I bent over you
a wealth of gifts poured down,
& it was my pleasure to brush your disordered hair
      & bestow secret fruit on your ungrateful sleep
       with hollowed hands;
And how often you drew in your breath

[15]

with rare movement,
and I was falsely fearful lest you feel
the unwanted weight of nightmare
or strange incubus,
Until the fluctuating shadows
running before the moon
through the window,
persistent moon,
lingering wheel of light
touched your eyes and opened them;
And then, an angry speech,
elbows propped up
on the soft couch,
"So you return,
strike home to our bed again,
but only after you were expelled
from some girl's door.
And where have you spent
this long night of mine
now that the stars grow faint?
Damn you,
may you lead the sort of night
that I am forced to,
you debauched drunkard.
I led sleep astray
weaving a rhythm
at the loom
& tiring of that
took to the lyre & sang
my abandonment and your lingering
with a strange lover,
until
soft winged sleep
darkened my cares
among tears."

4

Bassus, why do you praise
  so many young women,
    trying to turn me from my mistress?
Why not accept it? I will stretch out
    the remainder of my life
quite well pleased with my thralldom.
Iterate, if you please, your praises
    of Antiope's figure,
      & the beauty of Spartan Hermione,
      & whatever lovely women
    adorned ancient generations;
for Cynthia's name will not be engraved beneath theirs;
    and lesser figures cannot compare with her;
  Not even the worst judge
    would be so odiously wrong
      as to dissent in this matter.
But corporeal beauty is the least of all reasons
    for the blaze of passion;
there are greater things
for which I would perish, die with pleasure;
  the native glow to her complexion,
    her lovely skills
    & ineffable delight under silent cloak.[3]
The more you would unbind our love,
    the tighter you pull the knot;
and your enticements
  will not go without retribution,
    she will learn of it
& she will be no silent enemy;

---

[3] "But corporeal beauty . . . cloak." In this passage Propertius, quite
typically, assesses Cynthia's physical charms as both her least and great-
est virtue.

she has an angry and busy tongue,
   & you will be held dear under no lintel henceforth
& your company will then be
      most unwelcome
        & forbidden to me.
Indeed at no altar will she fail to curse you
      squeezing hot tears from her eyes,
    however sacred the altar stone be;
  for no ruin enrages her more
    than the god departing, & love cloven;
      our love most especially.
And may she remain this way always;
   I ask it of heaven;
  and may I never find in her
    any cause for sorrow.

5

Exercise some prudence
      in your envy,
   & mute your troublesome cries;
   Leave us alone on our present course.
What is it you want,
      to know the fires of lunacy,
      to feel the worst of evils,
   & leave your tracks among hidden coals,
      & choke on a poisoned elixir?
She is not at all
   like your usual vagrant girls;
      adamant fury is her custom,
   & even if she abstains from cursing you
      at her altar,
   she will give you a thousand anxieties,
   & you will have no sleep,
      she will not take herself from your eyes.
She can shackle more turbulent spirits than yours,
    & you will beat frequent retreats to my door,
    & your virile oratory
      will fail with stammering,
& a trembling fear will shudder from your bitter tears;
    terror will transform your face,
   and whatever words you wish for will abandon you
      in the middle of your complaint;
and you will lose track of your whereabouts,
      & your very name.
   But thereby you will learn
      the weight of my chains
& what it is to walk away
      excluded from her house;
and you will no longer be so astonished

       that my face is pale
    & my body wasted.
Nor will your worthy ancestors come to the rescue,
    for love forgets to honor antique phantoms.
If you give her some small sign
          of indiscretion
   how quickly your once fine name
       will be common noise in her ears.
I will not be able to console you
   when you come looking for me,
      for there is no cure for my own wounds,
but you will share my discomfort in equality,
    & you may weep on my toga,
        if you return the favor.
Therefore give up your wish, Gallus,
    for when she brings you the answer to your prayer
    she will bring you more pain than you bargained for.

6

No fear deters me
        from cruising the sea with you, Tullus,
    no terror turns me from bending sail
        into salty Aegean wastes;
I would climb mountains in your company,
        penetrate Memnon's kingdom.
But Cynthia's words, her grave prayers
        & her pale lips
                enforce my lingering;
        her arms encircle my neck.
Her shrill voice,
        a fire in the night,
    cries that the gods have ceased to be;
and she refuses me,
        & counters my anger with menaces.
I cannot endure such complaining,
            not for an hour.
To hell with any man who can love in apathy.
Is it really worth it,
    to tour scholarly Athens,
            or behold the riches of Asia?
Is it worth bringing down
        a clamor of revilement,
    making her mar her face
        with crazy fingers;
        is it worth her declarations
    that she owes that wind kisses
        which moves against me,
    and that there is no evil worse
            than a man unfaithful?

You, Tullus, ought to try
    to rise to your uncle's glory,[4]
        and restore old laws among our forgotten allies.
You passed your youth without Amor,
    your loves being arms & the fatherland;
and may Eros not bring you
        into toil like mine,
           may he not enmesh you in such tearful affairs.
But allow me
    to remain in these prone circumstances
        that providence has decreed for me,
      & to abandon my soul
        to whatever wanton measures she might wish.
Many have ruined themselves freely,
        loving too long,
& may hell receive me still among that number.
I was not born to swordplay & glory;
    the Fates rule that I subtend Love
    as my exclusive service.
Whether you walk over
    yielding Ionia
      or where the liquor of Pactolus
        dampens Lydian earth;
    whether you go afoot by land
      or by sea with oars to your agreeable office,
If, then,
      at some future hour
      you think of me,
    you may be certain
    I live under this same bitter star.

[4] It is not clear what the glory of Tullus' uncle was. H. E. Butler
(Loeb translation) makes him proconsul of Asia.

7

While you speak your appointed piece, Ponticus,
     the affair of Thebes;
  song of cold steel
       between brothers—
  inviting comparison, if no evil come of it,
     with ancient Homer, the master himself
(if only the fates go easy on your efforts)—
I meanwhile am always agitated
       patching up my affair,
   looking for some sign
     from my unbending mistress,
and I am bound over less to genius
       than to pain,
  & I sing the hard moments
     she gives my manhood,
  & to this measure
     I polish out my years;
but it's where my fame lies,
     & may my name go down forever
       with these songs.
Let them laud me only
   in having pleased
     the learned young lady
  & in having borne up
     under her unjust attacks.
Hereafter let lovers neglected
     read closely,
& do well in learning from my troubles.
And you also, Ponticus,
     should you be brought down by Eros
       from the homing true curve of his bow
(though may the gods' scroll

roll out no such doom for you)
then your distant ramparts
and your far-marching armies
will vanish in oblivion, from then on neglected;
And you will wish
to bind down more supple verses
without much luck,
love being insufficient
to lift up its own canticles;
and you will then take great notice,
& I will seem no mean versemaker then;
indeed you may have me at the head
of that whole not ungifted pack,
and I do not think
the young will stand mute
at my graveside,
but they will call me
the poet of their flame
who lies there.
Beware of hauteur, epic poet; despise no love songs;
Love coming late is dearly bought.

8

Are you undetainable by love
      & my disquiet, madwoman,
        or do you long for frosted Illyria?
& is it your heart's desire
    to sail under the first wind
          to join this superb gentleman,
          whoever he is?
Have you considered the passage,
        the wind's force
& the sea's rumble,
    the board bench to sleep on,
      the pain of the hoarfrost
        gnawing your pretty ankles;
And how will your lovely frailness
        serve you
    as strange snows drift down around you, Cynthia?
I pray that the season of ice be doubly prolonged
    & the Pleiades detain themselves
      below the horizon
& the seaman's tackle lie idle;
May your moorings
        stay knotted to their post
      by the water's edge in Tuscany.
And may no ill wind dissipate this prayer;
yet should that wind rise,
    may it carry your sails
      safely forward
        in the running sea
though I stand alone on an empty beach
    with pain in my heart—
look back on my clenched fist then,
      O woman of benumbed sensibilities.

You have lied to me, & you deserve no goodwill
　　　　from this quarter,
　but still,
may the gods guard your ship
　　　　& your oars beat with good fortune
　　　past the Ceraunian headland,
　　　　　　& get you to Oricos safely.
As for me,
　no girl can entice me away.
　　　　You are my life,
& I will remain at your lintel
　　　　in bitter mourning,
nor will I leave off asking sailors
　　　your whereabouts;
You may go beyond Scythia, Cynthia,
　　　but you remain my love always.

8a[5]

She remains here
    oath & presence
      & I have won;
Let the disgruntled go hang.
    She couldn't withstand
      my assiduous prayers;
    The covetous & envious
      must now forsake their joy,
        my Cynthia forsakes the new way.
I am yet her love,
    and for me,
      she loves this city also,
      & she says that without me
        no realm might delight her.
She chooses to lie with me
    in my narrow bed,
      and she would be mine alone,
        no matter what;
    even without the rich emoluments
      to be found in ancient kingdoms
    or gold in Elis
      to be got from horse racing.
Whatever fortune *he* might give,
      or promise to give,
    will come to nothing;
not even her respect for profit
      will remove her from the folds of my cloak.
Not by gold
did I twist her into this orbit,

---

[5] Although there is no break in the manuscript, I.8a is clearly a separate poem.

nor by Indian pearl,
    but with the offering of alluring song.
The Muses rule over love,
       & Phoebus is never far from love,
    & I rely on these gods
      in my affair
    & rare Cynthia is mine.
Now it is allowed me
        to lift my new bough
    to heavenly reaches;
She is mine by day,
   she is mine by night,
    no rival will break and steal
      a love so strongly bound;
& this present glory
     will be acknowledged
      until my white old age.

9

I told you your time would come, love-mocker,
    & now you are no longer at liberty
        to bestow fine words so freely,
& you lie supplicating and pliant in her hands.
       This new-bought concubine exercises now
      a queenly dominion.
The priestess-oracles of Zeus
      cannot speak with more authority
        than I can
   as to which girl
     will snare which bachelor.
I have some skill, some experience, in these matters;
     I have felt the ache,
        looked through the tear-shadowed eyes.
Would to god I was still a stiff & clumsy novice,
    my burden of love laid down;
   what comfort is your solemn anthem
       your lamentation at the lyre-raised walls
      of Thebes brought down?
Mimnermus is better than Homer
    in matters of the heart.
Soft love demands a polished tune,
   so go and put aside your somber books
     & sing the song she wants to hear.
The notes might be different
    if you lacked this abundance—
      why go thirsty in the flashing stream?
If you tremble now,
    what will you do
when passion's full fire consumes you?
     These are the first sparks only;
    you will burn

& be left in ashes.
If you but knew, you would as soon
  face an Armenian tiger, or chain yourself
  to the wheel of hell,[6]
   as feel the blade of love in your loins,
   & lie unable to refuse her anything
    when she is angry.
A lover's itinerary is demanding,
  & Eros is not on your side.
Do not be taken in by her easy contentment;
  you must mount her with ever more vigor
   to keep her yours,
  and the gleam in your eye must be for her alone, now,
  and love allows no night not spent with her.
O Ponticus, abstain from the game
  of whispered seduction;
If your soul were oak or flint
  you might still be the loser,
  & your spirit is somewhat ethereal.
You failed to see
  Eros lurking in ambush,
   & now you are caught in his bone-cracking grip.
But admit it—
  & to speak of your passion
   may perhaps ease it.

[6] See IXION in glossary.

Gallus, I was with you
    when Eros first drew you among his delights
        as you reclined amid tears,
    a joyful sensual night;
the mere remembrance pleases me,
    & I pray for you in its memory even now,
that night when your arms encircled her
      & I saw you linger, Gallus,
and string out the silences
      between your words.
Voyeur of your dalliance,
    I could not leave you then, though the moon
      reddened in decline
& dreams slid against my eyes,
    such was the fire in your whispers.
You trusted me then;
    let this be your reward for pleasure confided.
I have kept your pain hidden,
    but there is greater loyalty than that.
I can fuse broken loves,
    draw open her folding doors;
  I can heal new love wounds;
    the cure rides with my tune.
I have not walked in Cynthia's love for nothing;
    She has taught me what to do
      & what to beware of.
Don't quarrel with her
    in her sadness
and speak not too proudly
    nor too seldom.
If she cries for some favor
    neither scowl nor refuse it;

and when she speaks kindly
     make sure her words
       don't fall in a void.
Despise her, & she will stir with anger;
  Hurt her feelings, & she will never forget it.
But if your pride recedes,
     and you throw yourself under love's jurisdiction,
      then she will yield up joy to you.
Choose not your freedom
     & a desolate heart,
  and remain in delight with one woman.

11

You [7] idle at Baiae
    Eye the sea
        & the lagoon built by Hercules,[8]
& I spend my nights
        thinking of you
           although that fact may have escaped your notice.
Does your love recede with distance?
      Has some enemy of mine
        counterfeited the flame
          & taken you from my songs?
May you lie at ease
      in a bay-borne skiff
& may you swim leisurely
    in the small lagoon
      hand over hand
   through low and yielding waves,
But may you not
    lie voluptuously
in the rustle of soft whisperings
      on the quiet sands.
The common stain of falseness
      often follows a girl on her own,
        she being unmindful of love's usual icons.
Not that I doubt you.
    I know your renowned reputation,
      but by the sea at Naples

[7] In this poem, as in others, Propertius moralizes about Cynthia, expressing a desire that she be chaste. Although his concern may be genuine, had she followed his advice and abandoned the life of a courtesan he would have had a good deal less to write about.

[8] Hercules' lagoon is the Lucrine Lake, said to have been formed when Hercules built a causeway at Baiae on the Bay of Naples.

Eros should be greatly feared.
Therefore pardon me
if my books have wounded you,
charge it to my anxiety,
Neither mother, home, nor kin
holds me as you do,
You are my life and home,
my continual delight,
I have no other care,
& when my friends run across me sad
or find me joyful
I may say you are the cause.
Amuse yourself no longer
in a decadent resort
whose waters drift lovers apart
& whose beaches
spawn accusations.

12

Why do you pretend
  I lack interest,
  O gossips & watchers of Rome;
    why level this accusation of apathy
    as the reason that our love hangs fire?
She lies as far from my bed as the Po
    lies from the river Don;[9]
She no longer coils around me
    as she used to in her love
    in bare-breasted embrace.
Her whispers only echo in my ear now,
    & have lost their sweetness—
    yet once I pleased her—
in that time none loved as we did,
  none loved with such fidelity.
I fear some evil eye was jealous,
    some envious spirit undermined our love.
  I wonder
    what herbs
      from high mountain meadows
      were the divisive potion?
I am not now
    what I have been
    and wayfaring may change any girl,
    and the greatest love
      is a diaphanous thing
    in danger of disappearance.
And now for the first time
I know the length of the empty night;

  [9] The Don, though not a literal translation, conveys the idea of great
distance.

the only voice is my own
hanging somberly in darkness.
Any man
who has a girl present to cry out to
can be thankful,
even salt tears please Eros,
& if a flame dampened can be rebuilt elsewhere,
Love finds servile pleasure
in such altered ardor.
But I cannot break our covenant
or love another,
for Cynthia was my first love
& will be my last.[10]

---

[10] Cynthia was obviously neither Propertius' first love nor his last, but, so far as is known, she was his greatest love.

13

I expect the usual thing, Gallus,
    your usual untempered glee
that my affairs lie in shambles,
    my love riven from me,
      leaving a lonely place in my life.
But I won't mimic your gibes;
    I wish you luck instead;
      may no girl cheat you.
But even while your notoriety spreads
    (for never lingering
      with the girls you ensnare),
      even now the blood leaves your face,
      even now late-coming love
      brings down ruin upon you, draws your feet
to her gate, then needles bravado
      with indecision, & you sneak off in retreat;
This the retribution, Gallus, for your callousness;
    one girl will avenge all those others.
No more girls from the streets now;
    she will welcome no recruit to your bed.
  I know all this
    not from any oracle, or any loose tongue;
    Can you deny my witness,
  that I saw her grow weak
    hanging from your shoulder;
that I saw tears lace your arms entwined,
    & saw you stammer after words
      to bare your soul?
And that I also saw what I can't modestly write?
Such was your passion,
    struck against frenzy,
      that nothing might have broken that embrace;

an embrace not incomparable with Neptune's
  when his desires tightened around easy Tyro.
No comparable flame enkindled Hercules in heaven
  when he first felt connubial joy
  after the deadly ridge of Oeta.
One night like that one pales all past flames,
for the firebrand she sets under you
  burns pretty robustly.
And she won't let you recover your pride,
  nor will she let you be stolen away.
A fire now moves you, & there is no marvel in it,
  she being worthy of Zeus,
  like Leda, nearly, & more lovely than Leda's child.
Her resplendence surpasses
  the old-time Argive beauties,
  & her eloquence would bring her any god.
Since love has beaten you down,
  use defeat to your advantage;
no other vestibule merits your worthy attendance,
  my dear Gallus, and she may overlook your errors,
  since you are new to this sort of thing.
So let her be the exclusive measure
  the only hope of your heart's desire.

14

Granted you recline voluptuously
    drinking Lesbian wine
      from a fine embossed cup
        down by the Tiber,
    and wonder at the swift-measured oar beat
      of the boats
    and at the slowly towed barges,
and though the forest emblazons the summit behind you
      like the Caucasus;
These attractions can't contend with love,
    which concedes nothing to riches.
For if she sleeps beside me
    & if we pass the day
        in the pleasures of the couch,
    then the very gold of Pactolus is mine,
      & the Red Sea's jewels.
Then kings must be second to me
      in my elation
(and may such joy endure
      until death reeves it off),
for with love adverse
    who can enjoy his money?
The rewards of wealth are of no account to me;
    if Aphrodite is cruel,
      she can wrack heroes
      & crack tougher hearts than mine.
Love will step past Arabian jeweled doorways
    & does not fear, my dear Tullus,
      to climb into the purple bed
& roll the unfortunate youth
      around in it in torment;

& then what good are colored weaves
of silken bed hangings?
And as for me
while joyous love is with me,
I won't waver in my disdain
for kingdoms & the gifts of kings.

15

I have feared your inconstancy, Cynthia,
    feared hardship from it,
but no such nefarious bad faith.
The turning of fortune puts me in pain,
    yet you pay no attention,
  offer nothing to allay my anguish.
And you sit here redoing your coiffure,
    after last night,
      idly prettying yourself,
admiring oriental pendants
    set against your breast,
  like a bride on her way to the wedding.
Now, Calypso wasn't thus "distraught"
    when her Ithacan set sail;
therefore her protracted weeping,
    a desolation of ocean around her,
      and she sat mournful, her hair let down,
  and damned the wide sea's injustice;
and she grieved for Odysseus,
    being unforgetful of the delights of the years past,
    though never after would she behold him.
And your distress
    is not like that Lemnian queen's
who remained without moving
  in the chamber Jason was riven from,
    consumed by love, hearing only the wind that took him,
    and she knew no love after.[11]
Exalted Evadne, glory of Argive virtue,
    went down to the flame of her husband's pyre—

---

[11] An allusion here to Alphesiboea, who killed her brothers after
they had murdered her husband Alcmaeon, has been omitted because it
seems out of place.

however no exemplary models
        could change your ways—
but your affairs might have been
        conducted more nobly.
Speak no more of it;
        your words renew lies, they anger the gods
        your neglect maligns.
But if chance brings you into evil circumstance
        you will regret the hard time you gave me.
        But that's hardly possible—the great waste of sea
        will first fall away, or the years run
        the other way, or love cease beating under my ribs.
Be what you want to, except another man's concubine.
        You should not degrade your shining eyes;
        for I believed your lies on their account,
        when you swore by them
        that if you lied you would put them out
        with your own hand. Can you lift up your eyes
into the high sun
        with no tremor? For you know your own lewdness.
For whom now does your face grow livid, and the tears
        glitter in your eyes? Eyes I have gone to hell for.
Believe these words, lovers, and not a woman's flatterings.

16

That door,[12]
  formerly thrown open to conquering heroes,
  gateway famous as Tarpeian virtue,
  entryway before which gold-worked chariots used to park,
  that door often anointed by tearful captive supplication,
now groans under the nightly quarrels of drunkards,
  and resounds to the pulse of worthless fists.
No lack, now, of dirty wreaths for the columns,
    & one can always find a few torches discarded,
      signs for the excluded.
But no gate can defend her,
    my mistress,
      from nights of infamy;
        that gate now subject to obscene songs.
Nor does Cynthia renew her good name
    and abstain from evil more exuberant
      than the dissolute age demands.
That door will be brought under bitterer lamentation
    by my stretched out night watch;
      I will never let those doorposts stand in silence,
        no song of enchantment resounding.
"Janus crueler than my mistress
    why are you silent,
      the folding doors closed tight?
Why no admittance, love undisclosed,
    why no thought of giving in
      to the transit of my secret prayers?
Will no end be conceded to my misfortune,
    no end to evil dreams

---

[12] This poem is spoken by the door, an acceptable phenomenon in
Latin, but for the English version I have had the poet speak instead.

on a tepid threshold?
The midnight sighs
    as I lie there,
        as do the declining constellations
           & the air floating frost under the morning star.
Only Janus never laments men's pains,
    he answers nothing,
        on silent hinge.
If only my whisper would drift through a crack in the wall
      and strike & turn my mistress;
    then let her keep her heart armored,
      I doubt if she could,
    or keep tears from her eyes,
      or keep her breathing even.
Now she lies straining against more fortunate arms
        than mine;
    my words move with nocturnal winds.
That gateway, foremost cause
    of my misfortune,
    is unbroken by my gifts;
Janus, you have never been wounded
      by any words of mine;
    none of these drunkards can say the same.
I deserve not to go hoarse with long complaint
    and unquiet vigil
      in Hecate's realm.
I have spun out tunes
    with new verses
  in your service;
    I have planted kisses on your steps.
And I have often turned
      before your dingy columns
    & brought due offering
      with secret hands."

Thus my speech
   to which I added the other outcries
      used by wretched lovers,
those clamors rising
   like the birds of sunrise.
And that door is damned forever
     by its vice-ridden mistress
     & the tears of the poet.

17[13]

I should never have left her
    to venture forth seaward
    for now I exhort the kingfishers
        of the desert seabeach,
and the port of Cassiope
        will not greet my ship on time,
& my prayers and vows fall on unwelcome coasts.
The winds cut into a scream
            in my ear;
        they rage as Cynthia used to;
shall fortune never bring calm breezes?
    Shall this thin-sanded beach cover my corpse?
O Cynthia,
    ameliorate your harsh complaints;
    there is retribution enough
        in the night & slanting shoals.
Can you sit dry-eyed and and hope for my death?
    For you will never hold my ashes to your breast.
God damn the man who first
        set canvas to ship's mast
    and first made a road of the reluctant ocean.
It was less an affliction to struggle
        with the caprice of my mistress,
    who is a rare woman, though hard of soul,
        than to stare at the dark outline
    of these coasts backed by unknown forests
        & lift invocation to Castor, patron of seafarers.
Had fate buried me before I left
    and my gravestone stood a marker to our love,

13 This poem and I.18 sound more like fantasies than like true accounts written in the circumstances described.

[46]

then she would have thrown the sacrificial locks
on the funeral fire
and laid my cinders to rest with roses
and cried out my name in grief
and prayed to Earth not to lie too heavy on me.
But now, let the comely daughters of Oceanus,
daughters of Doris,
release my white sails
and lead me to a safe refuge,
felicitous escort
of a choir of sea nymphs;
Let them do that
if they have ever felt the wounds of love themselves.

18

A desert void
   & silence
      share my pain
with the west wind drifting
   in the empty grove.
Here may I sing
    my secret pain
      with no ear hearing;
the silent cliff shall not betray me.
Where shall I pick up the thread,
    the beginning of your present disdain?
Why have you taken
   to dispensing grief?
Lately, you loved me,
   now I stand outcast;
I would have you think
    on the justice of it;
      what enchantment engenders this mutation?
Is it the shadow of suspicion,
    do you consider me unfaithful,
you of nimble opinions?
    If so
  you might contemplate returning
    for I swear that no fair foot but yours
     has trod on my threshold.
I owe you rancor
    for this ache in my heart
     but I would not affront you
   in my anger,
it would only inflame you
     to an orgy of self-righteousness
   and cause you to cry

and your bright eyes to swim
with rolling tears;
Have I hung out too few signals
of my desire?
Have I seemed too little sanguine,
love unseen on my face?
The oak tree & the pine tree here
sacred to Pan
witness my love. They have heard the melody
in the shadow of their leaves
& Cynthia's name
is engraved in bark.
The number of cares your injustice spawns in my heart
is a secret of your silent entryway;
I am well adjusted
to your overbearing pride
your commands, etc.
I endure them without complaint
& I am rewarded now
with these cold hills
a rocky path
& hard sleep,
O godly fountain,
& my solitary outcry
accompanies
bright high-toned birds
only
but nevertheless
they shall hear your name repeated
Cynthia
as shall the forest
& the quiet rocks.

19

I am not afraid now
     of the shadowy afterlife,
   nor do I pine away
       thinking of fate's due,
            the ultimate bonefire;
But I do fear
     that your love's strength
       will not survive until my funeral;
this fear is deadlier
            than the march to the grave;
Eros has not brushed my eyes so lightly
     that love comes not into them;
         my dust will not settle
              unhindered by love, & forgetful.
The hero Protesilaus in dark hell
         was not unmindful of conjugal delight,
     and burning to caress her, his joy, with ethereal hands,
his shade returned to his ancient home in Thessaly.
   And likewise, whatever becomes of me,
     my spirit will be yours always;
       great love cannot be confined
                by the sands of doom.
If that choros of beauties
         plundered from Troy by the Argives
         should come to be with me
I would yet prefer your greater charms
              to their loveliness.
And however long old age
might delay our union
   (and may Tellus grant you old age)
       your bones will be met with tears.
And may an equal love live in your heart

as my own cinders glow;
Then death will not come bitter to me
whatever place it finds me;
Yet I am apprehensive
that you will disdain my tomb,
some iniquitous love urge you therefrom,
compel you to dry your eyes;
the best girl can be bent
by such insistent incentive.
But while it is given us,
let us rejoice
in still-living love
although all time
is not long enough for it.

20

This cautionary note, Gallus,
   out of continual affection
      (take care it doesn't drift
         as many things do
           from your mind)
that ill fortune not descend
      on your careless affair.
Your young man, the flame of your desire,
     is as pretty as Hylas, at least as glorious.
Whether you walk streams sacred & shadowed
                 in Umbrian undergrowth
   or the Anio cools your ankles
     or you promenade whatever prodigious coast
       or by whatever water meanders friendly,
Always watch out
   for enrapturing girl-spirits,
     nymphs hungry with desire—the Italian kind are as erotic
                     as any—
    so that you will not go desolate, lovelorn
among cliffs and cold lakes, as Hercules did,
    distraught on the hidden banks
          of the wild Ascanius.

The story has it
    that Argus once set his prow for Phasis,
      a long sea ride from the dockyard at Pagasa,
and, his ship past the Hellespont, he glided under the cliff face
    at Mysia to mooring,
   where all hands rested by calm seaboard,
    heroes bedding the soft sand with leaves.
& Hercules' young friend went inland, sent looking for water,
  & Zetes & Calais floated in desire behind him,

sons of the north wind,
Calais then over him, airy fingers, then Zetes;
trapped under their wings, his lips nuzzled
by fleeting breezes,
from below, he, Hylas, beat them off.
And the winds abandoned that pursuit,
& he became the hamadryads' windfall,
at Pege's well, down from the mountain,
liquid nymph haunt. There
wild apples hung under trees
visited by no man,
& lilies gleamed in ponceau fields.
In his fairy meadow Hylas plucked up flowers,
& then, leaning unwarned over entrancing water,
loitering to the lure
of his own image,
he cupped his hand, leaning on one arm
& his beauty's gay dazzle
struck with wonder
the burning dryad choros;
& they nudged him softly down,
dragged him down wellward;
Then the choked cry,
wrapped with water.
And Hercules called his name,
but silent air answered
from the steening.

The moral of that story, Gallus,
is keep an eye on him
your boy Hylas;
Never entrust a comely young man
to the tender mercies
of these prowling young women.

21

"You, soldier,[14]
    scrambling from our common ruin,
      sword cuts from Tuscany on you,
        eyes swollen,
        eyes turned on my groan;
I was with you—
    but bring joy to your parents;
      keep yourself alive,
don't bring your sister to tears
    knowing how I died;
how Gallus got through Caesar's swords
    to be cut down
      by some unknown hand.
Leave,
    keep the secret
      of my mountain-strewn bones."

[14] In this poem the dying Gallus, possibly a relative of Propertius, addresses a comrade in the army of Lucius Antonius, defeated by Octavian in the Perusian War of 41 B.C.

22

You ask me, Tullus,
   in the name of our friendship
what is my lineage
and where my home is.
If you know the graves of this country
   around Perusia,
   a place so deadly to the fatherland
      in civil war,
Etruscan dust so painful to me,
      where my friend's bones lie unburied—
I was begotten there
   where Umbria borders
      the rich and fruitful plain below.

BOOK II

1

You would know the source
    of these many engravings, these words of love,
  this book of supple words,
    words from the lips softly.
Neither Apollo nor Calliope
  sings in my ear,
but Cynthia's genius presides
    & shapes my songs.
If you would have her walk glittering
      clothed in Coan tunic
    this whole volume will be Coan-clothed.
If her hair falls in her eyes,
  I say her hair is splendid
    & she walks exalted
    & delights in my praises;
Or if her ivory fingers
    strike a song through the lyre
    I display suitable wonder
    at her artful touch on the strings;
Or if she directs her entreating eyes downward,
    & with flung-away tunic
      wrestles naked with me
  then our struggles will be
    a reborn Iliad;
Her delicate words and deeds
    flesh a great epic.

Maecenas, if the fates had appointed me
    to inspire armed heroes,
I would not sing of Titans,
    nor of mountain laid on mountain
      by skybound giants,
nor of ancient Thebes,
    nor the Trojan ramparts
      in majestic Homer's song,
Nor Xerxes' command that the seas merge,
    nor old Remus's kingdom
      nor the pride of great Carthage,
nor how Marius saved the day for us
    against the German menace;
But I would speak instead of Caesar's affairs,
    I would intone Caesar's wars,
      & after that I would sing Maecenas.
And when I would raise the song of Mutina & Philippi,
    graveyards of our citizens,
    & the clash of ships off Sicily,
    or the plundered hearth fires of the ancient Etruscans,
    or of Ptolemaic Pharos seized,
  as much as I strummed an Egyptian air
    & sang of Caesar dressed in mourning,
    conqueror of seven rivers & of kings
    brought chained in gold,
    & the triumphant bowsprits of Actium
    carried up the Via Sacra,
my muse would have your name woven in that tapestry,
    Maecenas, loyal in arms, loyal in peacetime,
      & Caesar's comrade.
But Callimachus has a narrow chest,
    cannot rumble with enough majesty
      for the godly songs,[1]

[1] The phrase "godly songs" replaces the Latin reference to one of
Jupiter's quarrels.

Nor can my diaphragm sustain
    the rough verses of Caesar's Trojan lineage.
Sailors spin tales of high winds,
      plowmen likewise discuss oxen,
         soldiers old wounds, & sheepherders their flocks;
& as for me
    I speak of coiling combat
      on a narrow couch.
To each his own tune, let each man
      polish out his day
        in the exercise of his proper skills.

—and if I remember correctly, she vigorously condemns
      other nimble girls,
    and because of Helen hates the whole Iliad.

It is one glory to die for love,
      another to enjoy the fruits of it;
      May this singular love's benefits
        be my great joy.
Even if I taste Phaedra's murderous potion,
    or if I die by Circe's herbs,
      or even if the fire under a brass witch cauldron
    warms a spell against me,
      even so,
        the woman has ripped away my senses,
    & they will remove me from her house
only at my funeral.
There are medicines for pain,
  and of pains
    only love loves no artful alleviation.
Machaon cured Philoctetes of his snakebit shin,
  & Chiron brought light to the eyes of Phoenix,
    & Asclepius the god

restored extinguished Androgeus to his father's
fireside,
& Telephus was cured by the same lance point
that bit him;
But if a man can remove this grievous love
from my heart
that same man can hand an apple to Tantalus
& dip water out of Danaïan urns, lighten
the liquid burden on delicate necks,
& that same man can unloose Prometheus from his cliff,
& beat off the vultures feeding at his belly.
Therefore,
when the fates demand back my life
& I become a name chiseled briefly in marble,
Then, Maecenas, glory & hope of our youth,
& my hope & glory also,
if by some chance your travels lead past my sepulchre,
halt your British war chariot with its carved yokes,
& read, as your tears break
the grave silence,

BROUGHT HERE BY ENDURING LOVE

2²

I was free, & had planned to live single
    & sleep in my bed alone,
  but this peaceful life was cheated by love—
    Why is a mortal woman so inhumanly beautiful?
Zeus, I can understand your secret loves
        in the old days.
Her hair is honey-colored
    her hands long and slender,
Statuesque, she moves like a goddess,
    like Pallas Athena before her altars
      breast concealed by the aegis.
Moreover, she is no less spendid
      than that demigoddess
        stolen from the marriage feast,
lovely prize of the centaurs;
  or the virgin Brimo
    who lay with Mercury by a sacred stream.
Indeed the immortals should concede,
        even those who pulled off their tunics
          for judgment on Mount Ida;
Let old age never change her beauty
      even if she should live as long
        as the prophetess of Cumae.

2 W. B. Yeats has translated a fragment of this poem.

3

You, Propertius, bragging yourself invincible,
    have now tumbled into her pit,
  your proud spirit captured,
    trussed to your own desire.
Every month some new alarm,
    and now another book of disgraces.
A fish might come out & stroll on the sand,
    or a boar take to the sea,
if I were able to pass the night
  in the propriety of study.
Love may be put aside
      for a little time,
 but not cured.
It is not her fine ivory beauty
    that seizes me
  (although no lily compares with her,
    & her complexion is like rose petals
      floating in milk,
  like snow & Spanish cinnabar)
nor is it her hair
  flowing light over her neck,
    nor her bright eyes
      which sparkle in my soul,
  nor the Arab silks she walks lit by;
I am not so frivolous as that;
But with the cups thrown down
    she dances like lovely Ariadne
      leading the bacchanalian choros,
and when she strikes up a tune
    with Aeolian plectrum,
her lyre equals a goddess's, a muse by her fountain;
  Her graven verses rival those

of antique Corinna,
    & if she reckons her songs as fine
        as Erinna's were,
            can she be far wrong?
Candent Amor sneezed a bright omen [3]
        at your birth, Cynthia;
    the gods assembled your virtues,
    don't think you got them from your mother.
Such gifts are somewhat inhuman;
    ten months are insufficient
        to bring them to light.
Born the greatest glory
        of Roman womanhood,
    you are most likely, of our local beauties,
        to be thrown into bed
            by a god.
You will not frequent
    human beds exclusively.
    Helen returns to earth again,
    should I wonder if our young men kindle?
Troy, you would have gone down
        in more splendor for Cynthia—
once I wondered why war gathered
        below Trojan breastworks,
    why Europe came to Asia
with sword & spear
    in the cause of a woman,
but I see now why Menelaus demanded,
        why Paris refused to comply.
A woman's loveliness
        was a worthy reason for Achilles' downfall
        & Priam's gamble with his kingdom.

[3] Sneezing was considered a good omen.

If some artist
    would outdo the ancient masters,
      let my mistress be his model,
        & inspire his brush;
His work would burn Aurora in the sunrise
      & Hesperus at sundown
          with the fire of envy.
And should I break loose from her,
      may I fall in love elsewhere,
        & thus expire in sharper pain.
The bull first balks at his yoke
      but then accustoms his strength to the plow,
and a young man loves first
      with struggling emotion;
    but he learns love's poise in time,
   learns to bear love's bondage,
    as Melampus wrapped in dirty chains,
        chains of a cow thief, learned to endure,
his peculation being for love, not gain,
    for beauty,
      a beauty soon a bride
            in Amythaon's hall.

4

Often, often,
   you must first complain
      of her own delictions,
Often you must ask
    & often go with favor denied,
   and often gnaw your fingernails
      without good cause,
and too often hear your own feet moving
      pacing out anger & doubt . . .
My hair reeked of unguents,
    but to no effect,
   & my slow walk was a measure of vanity;
In this affair
   no herb-blade potion, no witchery by night,
     no grasses burnt by Perimede's hand
      have any strength,
for here causes are indiscernible,
     no stroke flashes in the light of day,
it is a dark road these evils ride on.
The stricken man
   needs no physician, and no soft bed,
   it is not the season, nor a cold wind
      molesting him—
He walks forth—and then surprised friends
    discover him suddenly cut down.
Whatever love is, it walks invisible
    & unforeseen.
But for what lying oracle
     am I not a prize catch?
And what old woman has not heard
     my turning dreams ten times?

Those who will love women
    are no friends of mine,
        let my friends take their pleasures in boys
for thereby you come down the flume
      in a safe hull;
small waves on a small beach
    float no man to ruin;
one word deflects his anger,
    whereas she
  will scarcely be satisfied with your blood.

5

Rumor idles through Rome, Cynthia,
   with the word of your whoring;
Had I deserved this, I might have expected it,
     but you will grieve in your turn, my love,
I will leave this place,
   slip out seaward
      with the first good wind;
I daresay one
  from the world's deceitful girls
   will rejoice in being
      the beacon of my song,
    & will neither use me so badly,
      nor dance on my feelings,
       & will notch her sharp words only for you, Cynthia.
Too late, then, your eye-glitter of tears,
   for black shadows hover
      over the long day of our love.
Now is the time
  to walk apart
   while the rill of anger runs,
for I know my present discomfort
    is a forecast of love's return.
My god, the waves of the sea
   aren't as variable
     under a fresh north breeze
as lovers are, wavering with soft words after anger,
   and storm clouds change less quickly
     with the precarious wind out of Africa.
Twist free from your unjust yoke
while you can, Propertius;
   the first night is the hardest,
    after which love's pain

begins to abate a little.
But may the mild rule of great Juno
    spare you from real harm, my love;
may you come through unsinged
    by the fires in your heart.
  The anger of the horned bull
    is not the only anger;
      there are softer replies to injustice.
I would not rip the clothes from your deceiving beauty,
      nor will I break through the door now shut
      or lay hold of your pulled-back hair in anger,
    nor would I trace the marks of my knuckles on you;
      I leave that to louts undeserving
      of ivy wreaths in their hair.
But I may pen a verse or two,
    & they are hard to erase,
"Cynthia of radiant looks & light words,"
      and although you dismiss your murmuring detractors
      in contempt
perhaps my art will bring a paleness into your face at last,
    perhaps a song will return you the pain.

6

The chamber of Lais
        wasn't comparably manned
        & all Greece lay prostrate
before that sliding door;
    And Thais knew no such crowd,
        Thais in whom
        the men of Athens took their pleasure,
Nor Phryne, whose profits might have raised new walls
        for blasted Thebes.
There are too many
        of these pretended kin of yours
        gleaning these familial kisses;
    and these ephebe portraits injure my eyes,
        & the names going with them resound
        with the pain of jealousy in my ears;
Cradled boys alarm me, & your mother's kisses are wounds,
    and when some woman, some sister,
        passes the night with you,
my fear suspects a man under the tunic.
This damned jealousy, this burning flaw,
    has opened great wars, so history has it;
It laid proud Troy in dust;
    the same bitter madness goaded the centaurs
        to war at wedding feast,[4] grinding chalice
                                underfoot.
And closer to home, Romulus,
    suckled with crude bitch-milk
left the Sabine rape as his example to posterity,
    & now Eros dares any crime in Rome.

[4] The reference is to the abduction of Ischomache by centaurs at her wedding feast.

Blessed are Alcestis & Penelope,
  & any woman loyal to a man's gatepost.
Why all the shrines to chastity,
    if any girl will walk where she wishes,
      if any bride may choose her occupation?
And these painted spectacles on our Roman walls
    are not eyed by our young ladies
        to no purpose;
no innocence resides in the gaze, or in the things beheld;
 folly and discord follow silent delight
    wrought by the painter's hand,
& may painters groan in hell for it.
   In old Rome
     no such discordant pleasures
      lit the beholding eye.
Not without reason
  has the spider veiled the holy places,
    Not without reason do the blades of grass grow long
     & wild in sanctuaries of abandoned gods.
And what may guardians prevent, if the girl is unwilling
        to be prevented?
No sour watchman may protect such a vestibule.
  But good faith is its own chaperone, Cynthia.
& as for me
  there will be no wife,
     no seductive young woman
       but Cynthia,
    my wife & mistress always.

7

Hers was a true delight,
 when that law was repealed;[5]
  that edict we wept over,
   our tears extended, the decree divisive.
But a love such as ours cannot be riven by any god,
 not Zeus himself.
"Ah, but Caesar is powerful."
 But his strength is in war,
   the scepter of conquest means nothing in love.
I would sooner lose my head
  to the executioner
than abandon this flame at a bride's will,
  or pass by your shut door,
   a married man
with a damp eye, your lintel forsaken.
What dreams would my flute sing to you then,
 flute sadder than funeral tuba?
My blood will cede no soldiers,
  but if I might follow your one true camp,
  even Castor's great horse
would not be a suitable mounting.
For only in love, indeed,
  did my name deserve to be chained to glory,
   glory borne beyond Caucasian snows.
You alone please me, Cynthia,
 let me be your singular pleasure also,
and your love will mean more to me
   than the title "father" ever could.

---

[5] A law requiring Roman knights, a group including Propertius, to marry had evidently been passed and then repealed. Propertius could not of course marry Cynthia because of her lower social status.

8[6]

You will not have it, friend,
    that the tears melt from my eyes,
        when love out of time past
            is stolen from my arms?
Love spawns the bitterest hatreds;
    I would be a milder enemy
        if he wished merely to cut my throat.
How can I behold her
    against other arms;
        Cynthia lately mine,
            called mine no longer?
The turning of all things
    curves love awry;
        You must stand victor or loser
            in the circle of love's wheel.
Great lords & tyrants bite the dust;
        High Troy & Thebes
            have been thrown down.
What gifts I gave, & what great songs I spun;
    but this brazen girl never spoke,
        never said "I love you."
Have I casually borne
    too many years
        a woman without probity
            and her household?
Have you ever thought me a free man, Cynthia?
        Will your high words ever fail at my ear?
Propertius, will you expire in the best part of your manhood?
Is there no precedent?

[6] In the Loeb edition II.8 has been rendered as two poems, but it seems
to me to be one poem, as in the manuscript. The break after line 44
indicates the omission of lines.

Didn't Haemon join his bones
with miserable Antigone's,
his own knife under his ribs?
He could not go home without her.
Pass away then, Propertius,
& let her rejoice
that I leave men's company.
Let her censure my shade,
& chatter at my ghost,
& dance over the funeral coals;
let her tread on my bones.
But you deserve to go with me,
gore staining the iron.
Such inglorious departure would dishonor my name—
but it would be an equitable settlement.

.   .   .   .

Yet empty-hearted Achilles, his prize girl taken,
stopped work & carried his sword into hiding,
saw the flight,
the Achaeans flowing back by sea's edge,
saw the Dorian tents afire,
the torch of Hector gleaming among them,
saw Patroclus' formless corpse
abraded by blood & sand
fallen with hair outspread—
all on account of
a girl's figure.
This the fury
of broken love's pain.
With his plunder back,
then came Achilles' revenge—
somewhat late;

And he hauled great Hector
            after Haemonian horses.
Any astonishment is, then, unwarranted,
      that love is my proper conqueror,
            for I have neither the mother
                  nor the arms
      that Achilles had.

9

I used to be
  where he is now
    but with chance
  and in due season
    she will reject him also,
      and burn for another more.
Penelope lived inviolate
  through twenty years,
    a woman worthy of
          hotblood princely attention;
  She put them off by craft and skill
      each night loosening & undoing
          her day's weaving
  never expecting to see Ulysses
& growing old in her own house.
          And Briseis
clutching Achilles' corpse
    raked her white face with her nails,
      she, a captive,
mixed tears with his blood,
    Achilles laid out in the yellow shallows
        of the river,
    blackening her hair in mourning
          with ashes
  and with her small frame
      bore Achilles' large-boned body.
At that time neither his mother, nor Peleus,
          nor his bereft Deidamia
was at his side,
    but yet Greece rejoiced at her trueborn offspring,
      & war did not extinguish decency.
But you, you

cannot lie unoccupied in your bed
    a single night,
& cannot endure a single day alone, you shameless whore,
    and indeed you & your lover laugh
      as you sprawl in your cups,
    & jeer and make jokes at my expense.
And this man you want is the very one
    who first jilted & abandoned you;
May the gods make him your permanent affliction.
Is this the acknowledgment of my vows
          & prayers
    when death hovered close by your head
and your friends stood grieving around your couch?
Where was this lover then?
    And what if I had been soldiering in the East,
      or if my ship had ridden at mooring
        in the Western Ocean?
You lie and dissemble well,
    that being a thing all women learn.
The shoals of the Syrtes do not shift in a storm
      as quickly
    as a woman's love pact is broken in anger,
      no matter how trivial the cause,
    nor do the leaves fly in the winter wind
      with such abandon.
But I see that this intent of yours
      pleases you; I yield to it.
May Eros riddle me completely;
    the blood is on your hands,
      and great honor shall it bring you.
The stars and morning frost,
    and the door you once left open,
      all bear witness
    that I never loved anything in this life

more than you.
     And it remains so, despite everything;
     I will take no other mistress to my bed,
          & I will part company with Aphrodite,
          & if I have drawn out my years
               a steadfast and godly man
may the gods then grant
     that your bedmate
          become a stone in mid passion.

. . . .

As the Theban kings fought
     despite their own mother,[7]
     so would I with him, despite Cynthia,
providing I could divine beforehand
     a favorable outcome.

[7] The brothers Eteocles and Polynices killed each other despite the
pleas of their mother, Jocasta.

10

The time comes
  for a new dance on the mountain,
    a new rite on Helicon;
The time comes
  to chant horsemen under the hill,
    and I will now sing of battle,
        & squads of heroes, & Caesar's Roman camp;
And if my strength fails,
  still, a laudable essay
 To try the great song
       brings its own commendation.
In a man's early years, his tune is a love tune;
  let age sing of swordplay;
 War will be my canticle
   when Cynthia's beauty
    is well inscribed in my books.
I would now wear
   a graven frown
    & learn a new lute,
  my spirit rising from the low song
   taking strength out of heaven,
     for the work needs a booming voice.
Now the Euphrates rolls
  unguarded by Parthians,
   & Persia grieves to have cut down the Crassi;
India kneels before Caesar,
     & virgin Arabia trembles in her tent;
For Caesar's hand will soon menace
the rims of the wide earth,
   & I will follow along
    tall among camp poets;
   may fate reserve me that honor.

But when we cannot reach
            a great statue's pinnacle
        we lay our wreaths
            at the foot;
and so now, without means
            to lift up a crown of song
        I put my myrrh in the fire
            with the simple ceremony of poverty,
for my verses are not yet baptized
            in the fountain of Hesiod,
        but their tune still flows
        from the bright stream holy
            to Aphrodite.

11

Your song must wait
    on a new singer
    or else you will be suitably unrenowned;
Let him praise you
    who would lay down his seed
                without fruit.
The truth is,
    though you will hardly believe it,
        that these gifts of yours
        will be borne off with you
            on your couch
  on that bleak day to come,
   & no traveler
      passing by
       will see your white bones
  and know & compliment
      the shining mind
that once graced them with wisdom.

12

Would your wonder
        not prove him dextrous,
                that artist who first painted Eros puerile?
He first
        drew out the truth
        that love lives at the expense of judgment,
    and that great goods
                may be run through
                        for a fickle girl's love;
And it was not without reason,
        fitting the god out
                with inconstant wings
    to move lightly in the heart;
        And we are broken in the surge,
            and the bright air moves
                        in no sure direction.
It was not without reason,
        the barbed shafts depicted in hand,
                The Cretan quiver nestled beneath the shoulder,
        seeing how he strikes,
            & strikes before we safely see the menace;
        and with that wound comes madness.
The young god sticks yet to his youth
            & his bolts stick in my heart,
                but his wing feathers are ruined,
                no wingbeat leaving my heart;
                    his wars break through my blood.
But what delight is there
        to rage in my bones?
A prouder god
    would bring his sword
            into other hearts—

better to stain a virgin youth;
  for you lay your whip
      on a thin shadow,
    not on the man I was.
And if you bring me
    to absolute ruin,
      who then will lift up your song?
This light Muse within me,
        is your greatest glory, Eros,
    and after me what melody
      will celebrate her face,
  who will sing her hands,
    & what canticle
      will light the sloe eyes,
& set forth the slow footfall,
    of Cynthia, my beloved?

13

Like the bright arrows
     driven home in a multitude
        by Tuscan bowmen,
   the flaming missiles of Eros stitch my heart;
Eros orders me
  to walk under the oriflamme
     of the slender Muses
      & live in Hesiod's sacred grove;
Not so I might sing wild creatures
      down mountain valleys in Thrace,
        or float my lyrics among the oaks of Helicon;
But so I might astonish a girl,
      take her with my song.
Thereat I should be more famous
   with my art
     than Linus, lyre teacher of Orpheus.
I admire more than her beauty,
     nor is it enough
   for a woman to be of a pure & proud descent.
Let it be my joy to have chanted my verses
     reclining with a brilliant girl
  & for my meters to have found esteem
     in her hearing.
These things fulfilled,
     the public in its wordy confusion
       no longer concerns me
For I will be content with Love for a judge.
   If by chance
  she is peaceful
    and pleased at my poems
    I disdain then
      the hostility of the gods.

13*a*

Whenever, therefore,
    Death shrouds the faint light in my eye,
      proceed thus with the funeral:
Set forth, Cynthia, with no long retinue,
    walk without ostentation
      & without effigies;
let no sounding tuba
      fan a complaint
         in the void of my doom;
lay me on no ivory-foot couch,
    lay the corpse on no golden bier,
      set out no row of censers smoking;
Let only a short procession be strung out;
      a plebeian burial.
And in that solemn train
      three books will be sufficient wealth
         borne down to the queen of hell,
    and you will follow after,
      wounds on naked breast,
no weariness muting my name on your lips,
    and you will seal my cold lips then
      with an ultimate kiss,
and then bestow the onyx chest
    with its Syrian treasure;
& when I am cinders,
    by the flame set under me,
    lay the ashes in burnt clay,
    build no great sepulcher,
      & plant laurel on the grave,
      that the shade cover the extinction
      of the fire;
and inscribe this verse:

ONCE THE SLAVE OF ONE LOVE ONLY
HE LIES NOW GELID DUST

And the glory of my tomb
    will be no less known
        than Achilles' blood-stained mound.
And Cynthia, when you arrive at the end of things, remember
    come down this same path
        in death
    to this stone by my memory
& meanwhile,
        don't despise this grave;
    the earth remains alive to some little of the truth.
Would that one of the triple Fates
    had murdered me in my cradle;
    for why is the spirit kept
        only for the wavering moment?
In three generations of mortal men
    no man saw Nestor's winding-sheet,
        but if some Trojan archer
    from Trojan ramparts
        had brought short the far-strung doom
            of his old age
    he would never have seen the interment of his son,
& he would never have cried
    "Death, death, why do you loiter more,
        you come too late."
Yet lamentation for a friend gone
is not uncommon;
Love is the everlasting due
        of those who have now passed by.
Witness Adonis, in splendor stricken by the boar,
    in the high ridges of Idalia,
        a pretty youth laid out

in the mountain marsh,
and there
came the great goddess Aphrodite,
hair floating out in mourning;
But with neither effect nor reason
will you call back the silent shadow, Cynthia,
and bones are mute.

14

No joy equal to mine
  was Agamemnon's
    at fallen Troy's fruits,
& no such delight
      was sea-wandering Ulysses'
      beached in his well-loved Ithaca,
Nor was Electra [8] so pleased
  as she embraced the urn in tears,
    her brother thriving,
Nor Ariadne, seeing Theseus safe
    out of the threaded maze.
My ecstasies exceeded all theirs
    in the aura of our night's conjunction;
  such nights are reserved for gods;
    my immortality thus now assured.

Formerly when I went to her
  a shambling beggar
  she would abuse me after;
    worse than a dry spring,
    she would say.
Now, though, her iniquitous pride subsides,
  & she no longer toys with my feelings,
    but god how I wish I had known;
    the secret of no help to me now.
I am a burned-out shell,
    beyond help,
and the path was well lit,
    & I was blind,

[8] In Sophocles' *Electra*, Orestes, Electra's brother, came home disguised and carrying an urn supposedly containing his own ashes.

but no man sees well
    an erotic beam in his eye.
But then, this magic:
    return her disdain,
      and she will come in the morning
        though she turned you out
  the previous night.
And others came, & shouted, & rattled her door,
    but my supple mistress reclined in my arms,
a greater conquest
    than Parthia plundered.
She is my captured gold, queen, & victory chariot.
I will nail my gift to your column, Aphrodite;
    under my name, the carved verse:

    THE POET LAYS THESE GARMENTS
      AT YOUR ALTAR, GODDESS,
  FOR A WHOLE NIGHT, SHE TOOK ME IN

Now my boat comes to shore, O light of my eyes,
    a full ship, shall it break in the shallows?
If you change now, Cynthia,
    through any fault of mine,
      may the gods strike me down,
May I be struck down
    in your very chamber.

15

Ah, delightful night,
    radiant with joys
        couched in whispers;
Our hot whisperings of love
        burned under the lamp
        and how we rolled & struggled
when the lamp was darkened,
   & how we wrestled,
        her breasts bared one moment,
        the next putting me off with closed tunic.
And she nuzzled my eyes
    with her soft lips
    & reproached me for lying there calmly.
We exchanged embraces,
        coiling, uncoiling,
        entwining arms first one way, then another,
    and our kisses lingered in abundance.
No pleasure comes from blind twisting about;
    It mars lovemaking;
        the eyes should light our caresses.
Paris himself was brought to distraction
   at the sight of Helen naked
        coming from the chamber of Menelaus;
Endymion was naked when he inflamed the heart
        of Luna the moon, they say,
    and she came to lie with him,
        the goddess being nude also.
But if you will lie abed obstinately clothed
you will have your tunic torn off
        in my fist,
& further provocation, on your part,
    will earn you livid arms

to display to your mother.
Aging breasts do not yet
keep you from bedplay;
only women who have borne children
and are shamed by it
need be thus abstinent.
Let us satisfy our eyes with love
while Fate allows it;
The long night comes
for which the day will not return.
Let us lock in an embrace
that no day will come to sunder;
Let the coupled doves of Aphrodite
be our example.
To want the fire of passion to die
is wrong,
for true love has no fixed measure.
The earth will sooner delude the farmer
with a false bloom of spring
& sooner will the sun whip the black horses of night
across the sky
and river water run backward
and the abyss be parched
and fish swim thirsty
Than I would love any but Cynthia;
I will live faithful to her
& hers I will die.
As long as she yields such nights to me
a single year is a long life,
with many nights I would be immortal, even
with one evening a god.
If all men conducted their lives after my example
& lay down heavy with wine
there would be no brutal death by ship or sword,

our bones would not turn in the sea off Actium
nor would Rome suffer triumphs over her own
        & ache with mourning.
Certainly our descendants can say
        that our chalice wounded no god.[9]
Do not abstain from life's fruits just now
        with the light yet with you,
    give me all the kisses you can
        and that will still be too few;
   and just as drying-out garlands shed their leaves—
you see them floating
        strewn here and there in the wine cups—
so now lovers with high hopes
    may find the morning
        closing out their fate.

[9] This odd passage for such a poem—"If all men . . . wounded no
god"—says much about the poet and about the times in which he lived.

16

Your newly come Illyrian,
     your praetorian treasure,
          is of some concern to me as well;
I cannot applaud his escaping
          rock-shoaled Ceraunia.
Ah, Neptune, if you had heard my prayer
          what riches you would have had.
Now, the laden board & the banquet, without me;
     Now, her door is swung wide, in my absence.
But Cynthia,
     I trust your native quickness
          won't overlook opportunity,
an opportune harvest, or perhaps a shearing.
          Then, his substance yours,
               invite him to hoist his threadbare sails for home.
Cynthia attends
     no bundle of rods,
          & she cares for no accolade,
but she loves her boyfriends' togas
          or the fat wallets therein.
And from me, she wants Indian gemstones
     & demands gifts shipped from Phoenicia,
          demands them constantly.
I wish no man in Rome was rich,
I wish Caesar's palace was straw,
     & no woman up for sale;
     and then a woman's hair might grow white
          in one house.
And Cynthia
          would not
          lie down elsewhere then
     seven nights on end

polished limbs stretched out for so foul a man.
And I haven't wronged you
(you must grant that);
it is, rather, that lovely girls
will run lightly through a multitude.
And this barbarian, a coal in his loins,
paces before your gate,
& suddenly he reigns in my place.
O Aphrodite, aid me,
may his constant lust dismember him.
Can any man buy her,
enjoy bartered love?
Then by god she will be undone.
Remember how bitter were Eriphyle's gifts,
and how Creüsa burned in her bridal gown.
Can't my wounds be healed by tears
or will my pain bed down
with your vices always?
Some days have passed now,
in which I have had no heart for the theater,
or the games; and I rise up from a full table.
My shame, this great chagrin,
may it cure me of folly.
But perhaps love has no sense of honor,
perhaps lovers are shameless
& heedless of ridicule.
Witness Antonius, who lately filled the sea
with damned soldiers,
their cries hollow in the wave troughs;
ill-founded love leading him on,
turning his keels to the earth's rim,
a refugee.
(And it is Caesar's glory & virtue
that he conquered & laid away the gauntlet.)

But may I see all your praetor's riches,
  his robes, his emeralds, his golden chrysolite,
sucked off by a shrieking wind;
  May they turn into dust, or dissolve into water.
Zeus is ungentle with perjury in love;
  he is not deaf to prayer.
  You have heard the thunder splitting heaven,
  seen the lightning in the house of Aether.
These are no threats from the Pleiades,
  from rain-bringing Orion.
The god of Olympus has his signs of displeasure,
  & he once shed tears at a woman's guile.
Lying girls do not escape forever.
  You might remember the possibility of retribution
  & shed your Sidonian tunic [10]
  when the south wind blackens the sky.

[10] "Sidonian tunic." I.e., ill-gotten gains.

17

To lie, to break the promise of a night's love,
    is to stain your hands with your lover's blood.
I am the singer of these songs; how many times I have filled
    the bitter night with silence,
        an exile from your chamber.
May your heart beat less coldly
    seeing Tantalus with a dry mouth
        by an abundance of water
            falling away, enticing his thirst,
Seeing Sisyphus at his fantastic task,
    laboring behind the rolling boulder on the mountainside,
and seeing that a lover's road is harder,
    a fact the wise should know.
I once bore men's envy, but now
    the price of admission is a week's abstinence.
O I would get some satisfaction, my faithless Cynthia,
    leaping off a cliff, or taking fine-ground poison
        in my hands
now that we can no longer meet in the cross-paths of Hecate
    under the dry moon, & lie in repose,
    & I cannot whisper through the chinks in your door.
Ah, but for all these things, despite them all,
    I would not change you,
for the time will come when your tears will betoken
    some feeling for my faithfulness.

18[11]

Assiduous complaining
   spawns retribution;
      A woman often breaks on a man's silence;
If you have seen anything, build no quarrel on it;
     If you have been hurt
        deny the pain.

What if my hair should whiten
   & age web my countenance?
Aurora didn't disdain old Tithonus [12]
     in her eastern palace,
   she frequently embraced him hotly
     before she left with her horses,
   & as she lay limbs laced with his
      she complained of the cycling days
    as the sun came
& she decried Olympian justice as she mounted her chariot,
    and did quotidian duty in the world unwillingly.
Tithonus living was a compensation
     for her lost Memnon,
& it was the joy and pride
    of dawn's excellent deity
   to sleep with an old man
    & kiss his white hair.
But you would hate me even if I were a stripling youth,
   though you will be
    a withered hag
in the light of future sunrises soon enough.

11 This elegy, with unusually abrupt transitions, is presented as three
separate poems in the Loeb edition.
12 See Ovid's *Amores* for a quite different version.

BOOK II

Indeed the custom of Eros
to bring grief to those
whom he has treated well before
comforts me somewhat.

But you
even now you recklessly emulate
rouge-cheeked British girls,
you entice men to pleasure
with the gleam of foreign cosmetic.
The tinge of Belgian lipstick
on a Roman girl
is an odious thing;
the greatest beauty is always as nature made it.
Let evil overtake the girl
who deceives with dyed hair,
save a place for her in hell.
You can appear more truly beautiful to me
by appearing more often.
What of a girl who smears her face
with blue shadowing?
Can an azure face be lovely?

Since you have neither brother
nor son
I should assume their duties;
Always be fastidious
in the custodianship
of your chamber
& do not go seductively veiled
& ornamented.
You might avoid indiscretion,
for rumor walks by land & sea
& I will believe
rumors of your infamy.

[97]

19

You take your leave from Rome,
    though it is no wish of mine;
I am pleased only
        that it's a lonely country
        where you will be without me.
No seductions in those virgin fields,
    no flatterers drawing you from upright chastity,
    no commotion before your windows,
a sound sleep, with no acrid speeches
        on the other side of your door.
You will live without company
        & look out on singular mountains;
No amusements will divert you from rectitude;
    country temples [13] are not consecrated
        to your libertine rites.
You will see there
    only the drawn-out furrow with a bull at the end of it
        & the collapse of grape leaves
            before sickle swing;
You will bear thin myrrh
        to shrines little visited,
        offer a small goat to a wild altar's fire,
& dance bare-legged in desert places.
    May no man intrude on this.
And I
    will turn to the hunt, delight in Diana,
    lift up vows in her worship,
        and lay Aphrodite
            to one side,

[13] Lovers often met in temples.

[98]

& set snares
   for the untamed foot,
    offer horns to the pine tree,
  yell behind ravening dogs—
    but forgoing the lion chase, of course,
   & pursuit of the boar;
I am better suited to confront instead
   the subtle hare,
    & nail birds with reed arrows from a tight bow,
  where water veils the groves with light
   among shining herds in Umbria.[14]
But remember, whatever you do there,
   I will join you
  before Lucifer lights the morning
    too many times more.
Keep to the aforesaid things,
   and no empty forest
or winding creeks feeding through moss on long ridges
   will keep your name from my lips;
I would not wrong you in your absence,
   or be wronged.

[14] These two lines, although suggested by the Latin, are not a strict translation.

20

It eludes me why
   the hot tears mark your face
like Briseis bereft of Achilles
      & why you cry more bitterly
        than unhappy Andromache.
My god, you rave and beseech heaven
     to rectify my supposed unfaithfulness,
   & complain that I no longer love you.
          Why?
Why is it? The nightingale mourns with no such racket
       among the leaves in Attica,
  nor is haughty Niobe guilty
    of letting slide so many tears
      down the mountain,
    despite those 12 tombs.
Even if I were stashed away
    in Danaë's treasure donjon
     & my arms shackled with brass,
  yet for your benefit, my dear, I would sunder brass
      & break out of the iron tower.
I don't give a damn
    what others say of you
& I adjure you
      return the favor
  and doubt not my fidelity.
I swear to you by the sacred bones
    of my father & mother
—& if I deceive you, may their spirits exact a hard death—
that I will be yours until that final darkness;
   we will be carried off together.
If neither the luster of your name held me
    nor the glory of your looks

then I might yet be bound by your delicate ways.
   The full moon has risen in the night seven times
     since the lounging street-corner gossipers
     began their whispers of you & me,
     and in that time
     I have often been welcomed under your lintel
     & shown the pleasures of your bed.
I bought not one night with gold or gifts;
   whatever I have been with you
has been through your passion
     & I give thanks for it.
Many desired you, & you sought only me—
   can I forget such fire
     & such favors?
If it happens, may the foul Furies seize me;
     may I be condemned by a bleak judge to hell,
& gnawed by wandering buzzards,
     & may I labor without end
   on the hill under that slippery boulder.
Send me no more begging tablets;
     I will be as faithful at the last as at the beginning
& in this I am forever vindicated;
     Alone among lovers
I do not undertake love quickly, or rashly end it.

21

May Aphrodite devise
    as many evils for Panthus
    as he invented lies about me;
You must admit
    I fortune-tell as well as Dodona's oracle,
for your pretty lover has got himself a bride.
    Are so many nights passed away & lost?
Is your honor unruffled?
      Notice: he sings in freedom
      and you lie alone; you were taken in
        too easily.
And you are now a topic of their conversation,
    & it is his sneering declaration
      that you came to his house
      against his will.
May I be damned absolutely
    if he wants anything at all
      but the renown of having had you;
    No small glory for this bridegroom.
Thus strange Jason once cheated
      that girl from Colchis,
  ejected her from her house,
      Creüsa then installed therein;
And Calypso was deceived by a boy from Ithaca,
    & she later beheld her lover
      stretch out his sails.
You young women who offer too quickly,
    with only a whisper at the ear,
      learn, now deserted, not to say yes too lightly;
But already, Cynthia, you have begun
    looking for another;
    one who might stand more firmly.

BOOK II

Lunatic girl,
    caution can be learned in one easy lesson.
But for all that,
    I am yours, my love,
       in good health or in sickness,
         in whatever place,
           or whatever the nature of the times.

22

Once
  many girls pleased me equally
    & you know, Demophoön, that a good many evils
      came of it.
No crossroads bordello escapes my probings;
  I explore not in vain,
    & too much theater has ruined me;
Some provocative girl
  standing with her radiant arms outstretched
                 inviting
  her lips rounding out
    the rhythms of her songs,
And even then my glittering eyes
  search out my own undoing,
    & light on some gleaming attraction,
      some girl sitting with uncovered breast
      with an Indian jeweled clasp in her hair
      & a lock of hair down over her eyes,
And if she refuses me
  with a hard look
    cold sweat trickles down my forehead.
You ask, Demophoön, why I am so tender
  to one & all.
Love has no reply to such a question.
Why do Cybele's cultists lacerate their arms
  with sacred cutlery
    & slash themselves
      to the twisting cadences of the Trojan fife?
Nature fashions each man a vice
  & Fortune ordains continual love as mine.
Even if Thamyras' fate walk behind me
I would never be blind to beauty,

my envious friend,
& if you think me thin, & feeble in the joints,
you are wrong.
Serving Aphrodite is never too much work
but the question is allowable.
For often a girl's proving lasts the night
& I retain the power of my ministry until dawn.
Jupiter laid the northern constellations to rest
two nights on end for Alcmene
& the heavens were two evenings without their king;
But he did not return to the thunderbolt
languid from his labors;
love is always renewable.
When Achilles rose from Briseis' embrace
& went out, did the Trojans panic any the less
in the face of Thessalian lance point?
And when ferocious Hector walked forth
from Andromache's chamber
did not Agamemnon's fleet have good cause for fear?
Either man could bring down walls
and splinter ships,
& in love I am
as Achilles was, or lusty Hector.
Consider how the sun & the moon serve the sky,
& two hawsers keep a ship better
& twins are best for a worried mother;
Even so one girl is too few for me;
if one will not have me
another will receive me
& lie hot with me
with eager strength.
If one girl is angry
with my ministrations
she should know there are others waiting.

22a

You need not enter my door
  if your heart hardens against me,
    but come to me
      if you love me yet.
But why waste words?
    To be left waiting for one's love
      is a pain that penetrates the soul
   as none other,
   & how the victim's breath
    wracks him in his bed;
He refuses to believe she won't come
   & he fatigues the servant boy
     with that question
     with the unchanging answer,
   & sends him to verify
    the ill turn feared.

23

Quondam disdainer of the common way
      & paths of the vulgar unlettered,
Propertius now inclines
    to go with the multitude,
  to partake of the public tank;
That water is sweet to me now.
Should any freeman enrich
      his lady's slave boy
        that he might have words from her, in writing?
And be always inquiring
   whether her feet tread the Campus,
      and where on the Campus,
and "where is she now, in the shadow
      of which portico is she now?"
Then, after labors eloquent as Hercules'
    to get a letter:
"Have you no gift for me?"
Then it becomes your pleasure
  to return the knit-browed stare
     of some sour chaperone,
    & often then your captivation leads you
  to lie in secret
   in some dirty hovel,
a hell of a price
      for one night in a year.

But one may turn elsewhere;
there is that girl
   who strolls in liberty
     with her cape thrown back
     and no cloak of fear—
  is she not more

to your liking,
she whose slippers polish the path
in her promenade
on the Via Sacra?
No hesitation
when you ask her to come,
no delay,
and she is more demure in asking
what your astringent father has given you
(that gentleman who cries out so much
at your expenses).
Nor will she demand your instant departure
saying she is afraid
saying her husband returns from the country,
returns this very day.
Let these girls from Persia & Syria
be my delight;
I want no more of this furtive modesty
in my lady's chamber.
You have this choice only; love or your liberty
since no man may both love
and stay free.

24

"And you will say this,
     with your book gotten notorious,
     & your Cynthia inspected in the Forum?" [15]

Now, such words
     would break sweat onto any man's forehead,
     whether from embarrassed honor, or a wish
          that certain affairs remain unspoken.
But if Cynthia's breast moved close
     in her pleasures again,
     I would not be called Rome's chief prodigal,
          & have an infamous reputation
     making its way through the streets;
and however much I burned
     with misdirected lust,
I could at least manage
     to dissimulate in the matter.
But let no man be amazed
     that I look for cheaper girls
for they display a seemlier moderation
     in backstabbing.
          Does my reason seem fickle?
And as for Cynthia, at one moment
     she demands a fine fan
          of peacock feathers,
with the next she would cool her fingers
          with jewels; and she will risk my anger
          wheedling for ivory dice
     & whatever gaud glitters along the Via Sacra.
I will be damned

[15] In the rest of this poem, Propertius defends himself against this
anonymous reproach.

if the expense bothers me,
but it is the shame,
being an anecdote
in the career
of this treacherous woman.

24*a*

Was it your will, from the first,
  that I delight in *this*? [16]
Doesn't your face burn, my inconstant lovely Cynthia,
  when we consume one night in love
& with the next you declare me
  a burden to your bed?
You would go through my songs & extol them,
  & now does your light love
    drift off so quickly?
Let this other gentleman compete
  in talent or skill, & in so doing learn
to confine his desires to one house.
Of if you are amenable, try him, give him
  some Herculean test, [17]
or have him choke down whatever you would have him drink,
  seawater after shipwreck, or poison,
& abstain from no misery in your service
  (I rather wish your whispers demanded
    equal efforts from me),
  and then your bold friend might pale a little,
    who now slides into good fortune,
      swollen & boasting.
It will not last a year with him,
  but Sibyl's eons would not divert me,
  nor Herculean workouts,
    nor the black day at the end of things.
You will collect my bones, saying,

[16] Propertius is referring to one of Cynthia's many infidelities, which were probably more numerous than his own.

[17] The "Herculean tests" are specified in the original, but it is hardly necessary to reproduce them in English translation, where they would sound very strange.

"Ah, *you* were faithful, and never betrayed me,
though ordinary blood ran in your grandfather's veins,
    & you had no money."
Neither pain nor wound could change me;
    Your great loveliness is no burden,
        though I stagger under it.
Perhaps some few have perished for your figure,
        but I imagine more have victimized you,
    after certain examples;
for Theseus prized Ariadne—as far as Naxos,
    & Demophoön cherished Phyllis, for a time,
& Jason laid up safe in his hold
    deserted his enchantress finally.

But then it is a troublesome girl
    who will fit herself out for a crowd.
Do not gauge me against rich men, or the wellborn,
    for they would not come at the last
    to gather up your ashes—
as I would.
But I would prefer a prior departure,
    you sending me off
    with bare breasts
    & hair loose in lamentation.

25

My grief, my lovely sweetheart,
    a pretty pass we've come to
      when fate forbids invitation,
But I will make your splendor
    most notorious,
      with your pardon, Calvus, and your leave, Catullus.
The old legionary sleeps
    with laid-aside sword,
      & an old ox will no longer plow;
The rotting ship lies on deserted beach,
    & the ancient scarred shield stops dust
      on the temple wall;
But years will never desolate my passion,
    not Tithonus' age and not Nestor's.
Cruel Perillus, slave to a hard king,
    had it better roasting in his own bronzework;
and I would even prefer
    hardening at the look of the Gorgon
    or to suffer under the fowls of the Caucasus;
But I stand firm.
  The water eats away the blade
    and dissolves flint,
But no love that persists
    & bears undeserved insult
      is worn down by the lintel it waits under.
The lover supplicates when scorned
    & admits wrong when himself wronged;
      always returns with reluctant foot.[18]
But you, you puffed-up fool,
    while your affair prospers remember

---

[18] Up to this point Cynthia is being addressed; from here on it is her lover who is addressed.

women waver considerably, no woman is permanent.
Does any man give thanks
    while the storm hisses on sea-foam,
        when splintered keels float on lee shores?
Who demands the prize in mid race
    before the wheel grinds over the goal?
The hot winds of love
    drift and whip
        from unexpected quarters,
and love tripped up late is ruinous.
    While she yet esteems you
        confine your delight in a silent heart
    for lavish praises
            undercut love in unknown ways.
Enviable possessions are usually transient;
        Remember that while she still wants you.
If Cynthia were a girl pleased by ancient fashion
    then I would be where you are;
        I am defeated by current style.
But these times haven't changed my nature;
    Let each furbish his own path.
You who want too much
    will suffer pain
        like a needle stitching the eye.
You see an enticing white glamour
    or dark radiance;
        Either seizes and inflames;
Likewise the plebeian girl
    and the girl
        vermilion-cloaked;
    both wound the soul;
One woman is enough
    to bring nightmares out of the dark;
One woman is tribulation enough.

26

In that night, my love,
　　I dreamed a broken keel,
　　your tired arms splashing
　　　　in Ionian spindrift,
　　and heard your duplicity confessed,
yet you couldn't raise up your head,
　　long hair heavy in the sea,
　　　　like Helle turned
　　　　　　by billows shining purple,
that girl once mounted softly
　　　　　　on a golden ram.
I feared
　　you might become a name
　　　　on the sea's list,
　　another loss mourned by seamen
　　　　gliding in those waters.
Ah, what prayers I lifted then,
　　To Neptune, to the Gemini, & to Leucothoë—now a deity;
And hands awash in the sea-swirl,
　　you cried up my name,
　　　　as if you would soon slide under.
And if Glaucus had seen your eyes,
　　　　you would now be a sea nymph,
　　　　to the raucous envy
　　　　　　of the Nereides.
But a dolphin came under you,
　　　　came to your rescue,
　　　　　　the same who saved Arion from the sea-grip,
　　lyre & all.
But I,
　　in the meantime, had dropped
　　　　from the high cliff,
　　when panic broke the dream.

26a

Let consternation reign through Rome,
    that I captivate so great a beauty,
    let the news of her enslavement astonish them.
No "rise up from my bed, poet," from her,
    not for a Persian king [19]
    or a golden river; [20]
When my song enchants her
    she avows disdain
    for wealthy men.
And no girl honors the measured verse
    with rites so sacred;
Faith and steadfastness in love
    are worth a good deal,
    and the bearer of great gifts
    may expect a great return.
If she considers carving through the long sea,
    I will stay fast by her side,
    and the wind will slide us
    through the same waves;
    we will lie on the same beach
    shadowed by the same leaves;
We will drink from one well,
    lie together
    on a shipboard plank,
& I will stand against savage easterlies,
    endure cold cutting from the south
    slatting the sails,
and endure the storms that bruised Ulysses,
and jostled the Greek ships aground in Euboea,
    and the winds that broke through

---

[19] Cambyses is named as the Persian king in the original Latin.
[20] The literal translation of the Latin would be "rivers of Croesus."

the two cliffs [21]
    when the dove lit on the Argo
        to lead the way into the unknown sea.
I fear nothing,
    if she remains the light of my eye.
If the god of lightning enkindles our bark
    then the waves will wash us naked
        onto the same coast;
    or let the seas suck me under
        if the land may shield her.
But Neptune isn't hostile to Eros,
    being his great brother's equal
        in amorous disposition;
    Amymone will testify to that
        who in Argos knew the strength of godly embrace
            to break a dry season,
    when the trident struck in the swamp,
        & the god paid off his promise,
            a flow from a golden spring.
And Oreithyia, reft by Boreas from her home,
insisted he wasn't so bad, her plunderer, the north wind's god,
        who rumbles in mountain & high ocean.
Have faith, Scylla will weaken for us, & Charybdis,
        who drives her riptides endlessly in a waste of ocean.
No blackness will cut off the starlight;
    Auriga [22] will glint clear
        above bright Orion.
And should I give up my life,
    my body entwined with yours,
        I would prefer
            such a departure
                to any other.

[21] The two cliffs are the Symplegades, two rocks at the entrance to
the Black Sea which dashed against each other to crush whatever passed
between them.
[22] The Latin has Haedus, or the Kid, which is part of the constella-
tion Auriga.

[117]

27

In the clear skies of the night
  men seek to know
    which star gleams auspiciously,
    which shines evilly,
& they demand to know when and through what chance
  Death will come upon them.
We may run down Parthians by land
   or British pirates by northern sea;
Each course is fraught with blind menace
  and men fear for their lives in battle,
    for Mars bears a two-edged sword;
  Men fear fire and ruin at home
    and the poisoned cup at banquet;
And only lovers may expect death
      without the chill of fear;
Neither sword edge nor the cutting north wind
nor the sight of the ship of hell
    with dark canvas
      from the reeds of the river Styx
need cause lovers to tremble,
  indeed even after the funeral fire
    a woman's anguished cry
may call up her lover,
    a shaded vision
      from the darkness.

28

Zeus save her, I pray you,
    Do not stain godly hands
        with such evil,
           the death of so beautiful a woman.
Now burnt wisps of air move
    in a dry season;
   now the earth glows arid
       under the glimmering Dog of the night sky;
But no fire of heaven brings this fever,
    rather her own neglect,[23]
      her disesteem for deity
        at the root of it,
    as in the disasters of other lovely girls
      in times past;
Now wind & sea drown out her invocations.
    Has comparison wounded Dione,
      goddess envious of all competing beauty,
   or did you neglect Hera's shrine?
        Or slight the splendor of Athena's looks?
A sharp & audacious tongue
    is the frequent gift of pulchritude,
  and your words & loveliness
      work to your injury.
Death yawns close and dangerous,
    but an easier day may rise
      from this extremity.
The Nile was the water trough
    of the horned goddess Io
in her early years

---

[23] This line and the preceding one, together with some others, indicate that the poem was written after Cynthia had safely recovered from her fever.

but her fortune has improved.
  And Ino once strayed through the world,
      but now mariners implore the blessing
of that lady transformed, the sea nymph Leucothoë;
and Andromeda was put out in chains as food
      for the creatures of ocean,
      but renowned Perseus made her his bride;
And Callisto once
      rooted through Arcadia as a bear,
  whereas her stars
      now stake out the sea-lanes
      for night-filled sails.
If ill fortune carries you
            to the rites of the pyre,
then go and exchange stories with Semele
      of the perils of glamour and good looks,
and you will take the foremost place
      even among Homeric heroines,
& there will be no votes cast against you.
Prepare yourself as best you can,
      meet calamity with dignity
      though destiny strikes you hard;
and God & your funeral day
      may both be held off,
      and Hera herself may grant a stay,
for the pain of a comely girl's death
      is a knife even in her cold heart.
The magic-twisted rhombos [24]
falls silent, sings no longer;
  the altar flame drifts out,
      the laurel lies smoking,
& the moon now declines to descend from heaven,

[24] A rhombos is a bull-roarer.

and in the night
    from a dark bird,
a bleak tune
    hovering,
      a prophetic note.
But we will float together
    under the sails of the raft
on the indigo lake of hell.
    Pity us both, I pray, not one of us.
If she lives, then I may live also;
    should she fall, then I too will die.
I consecrate these words with a song,
    & I will dedicate these words

ALL-POWERFUL ZEUS

CHOSE TO SAVE   HER

& she will sacrifice
    & bow before the altar
& give thanks for deliverance
    from extended peril.

28a

Persephone, may your mildness continue,
Death, abstain from more cruelty,
    for your throne
    raises its shadow
    over too many thousands of lovely women;
Let this one remain here,
        aboveground,
it is not asking too much.
    You have carried off Iope
    & Tyro glows pale in your realm;
Europa is with you,
    & the dam of Minotaur,
and all those comely ladies of Achaea
    & of Troy the long-standing,
        the overthrown kingdom of old Priam
          & Phoebus Apollo;
And the ancient beauties of Rome
    are all gone among shadows,
        smoke in the consuming fire.
Beauty·is not long-lived,
    nor is fortune,
mortality awaits both.
But Cynthia, since you have come through this great peril,
    O light in my eyes,
    sacrifice to the Moon,
    reward the Moon with a dance & light a watch fire
        for your vigil;
Ten nights for the Nile goddess also,
        do it on my behalf.

29

In the evening late [25]
    ambling drunk
        without her, the flame of my soul
           & no hand of a servant to guide me;
    a stripling gang came from the dark,
        and fear shadowed my eyes
      seeing the torch glitter on the barbs
                of the arrows;
    and they came bringing chains
      & they came nude,
    and one lewder than the rest cried:
"Ah, the notorious poet, consigned to our tender mercies
      by the fury of his girlfriend. Grab him."
Then they put a rope around my neck,
    & I was thrown down among them,
      & when they were through
      one of them declared:
    "Don't think we aren't on a worthy errand;
      your mistress waited several long hours
        for an undeserving lover, a fool out
         sniffing around other doors.
But when she takes off her Phoenician gown
    & moves her heavy eyes
      you will breathe an odor sweeter
      than herbs of Arabia,
    an odor that is love's own work. Notice
We come to the house according to our orders."
    And thus with this escort
I returned to my mistress

[25] The original reads *hesterna*, "last night," but I have changed the phrasing to make it accord with the ending of the poem. Usually, as in the Loeb translation, II.29 is given as two poems, the second starting with line 32, "And the dawn had come."

once again.
"You should learn to pass the night at home."
And the dawn had come,
   & I wondered if *she* had kept a chaste couch
    & indeed she lay in bed alone.
And I was dazzled;
   she had never been more splendid,
    not even when she went before Vesta
     emblazoned in purple
      to narrate her dreams
   so neither of us should come to harm.
She shone in the radiant splendor of nakedness,
  & as she awoke she cried:
   "What? A spy
    with the sunrise?
Do you think I am like you? I am not so nimble.
   One lover is plenty,
    except I would rather have
     a better one than you.
However, you may notice that
  there are no traces of lovemaking in the bed,
   no signs of rolling about in the sheets
    or of two having slept here.
Note that my body doesn't heave with my breathing—
  you know well enough what the signs
   of infidelity are."
Having said this
she kept me off
  with her right arm
as I tried to kiss her
  & then she rushed off
   in her loose sandals.
Since then there have been no pleasant nights:
  my reward

30

as watchman of her fidelity.
What hardness of soul
rules these preparations
for a sea voyage
to shore dunes past the Hellespont?
Where will your madness take you?
There is no sanctuary
from what you run from;
Pursue exile into Russia,
you can't outrun Eros the god,
not even with the aerial wingbeat
of Pegasus saddled,
not even if Perseus lent you his shoes,
not even shot through broken winds
by wing-footed sandals.
The high Mercuric road
will get you nowhere.
Love stretches yet over you,
indeed over all lovers,
& bends heavy on once free necks.
And the god keeps
a sharp-eyed watch,
& once he has seized you
he allows you no proud glances
from then on.
But if you commit some peccadillo
your prayers can head off his anger—
if they are prompt.
Let hidebound ancient men decry love's banquet;
their ears are filled
with antique words;
let us, by this measure,
burnish the present path, my love.

In this place
　let the bone flute ring
　　which Minerva slid into the Maeander
　　　for swelling her cheeks.[26]
Shall I be disgraced, that I live
　contending peaceably with one woman?
If any crime is involved,
　it is crime at love's command,
　let no man reprove me.
Let it be your delight, Cynthia,
　to hold me softly
　　in rain-struck declivities
　on moss-backed ridges;
and there, you might see the Sisters [27] lingering
　in the high cliffs
　　where they sing the secret affairs
　　　sweet to Zeus in the old days;
　how Semele was consumed in his fire,
　　how Io's love brought ruin down,
　　　how finally the god came
　　　　in strange plumage to Troy [28]—
no human stands who could resist those wings,
　so why am I
　alone the accused defendant
　　in the common crime?
Let it not disturb you,
that those ladies look respectable;
　Even that choros knows

---

[26] Several lines of the Latin following this line are unintelligible in
the context and have not been translated.
[27] The Muses.
[28] Possibly a reference to Ganymede, who was beloved and carried
off by Zeus in the guise of an eagle.

what love is like,
if one [29] from among them truly lay
on the rocks of Bistonia
squeezed by her apparent boyfriend.
And when they put you
at the front
of the dance,
Bacchus behind
with his bright lance,
only then will I endure
the sacred corymb
dangling at my ears;
Without you
what is my genius?

[29] Calliope, with whom lay Apollo, disguised as her lover Oeagrus.

31

You demand to know
        why I come to you late?
Well, today I stopped for the grand opening
      of Apollo's magnificent portico,
built by munificent Caesar;
   a lot of Punic columns spaced out,
        statuary between pillars, a plethora of Danaïdes.
Inside, the temple
built of bright marble
(what god doesn't like marble?),
& at the two gables ran solar chariots,
   and the doors are worked in fine Libyan elephant tusk;
one depicts the fall of the Gauls,
      kicked off Parnassus,
the other displays Niobe's death;
And round the altar stood Myron's oxen,
    four cattle animated by the signature
      of the sculptor's art.
And in the shrine stood Apollo himself, lord of Delphi,
    in a long robe, between mother & sister,
     & in an attitude of song—
   he seemed prettier in marble than otherwise
        lips open to the silent lyre's tune.
(That's why I am late in coming to you.)

32

Sin alights in the eye
   of your beholder;
      desire resides
   in the eye's gleam;
You walk undesired
      only when you walk unseen.
Why do you seek out the quavering oracle
      at Praeneste, O Cynthia?
Why do you make for the walls of Telegonus,
   and drive your fancy chariot
      to Herculean Tibur,
& roll through the Appian Way to Lanuvium?
Better to walk here
      in your idleness,
but I cannot trust you
      when the crowd sees you go
        with enkindled pitch-pine
          light in the glade
      in Hecate's ritual.
You shy away, now,
      from the muck of Pompey's colonnade;
      you steer clear of Rome's coffled plane trees,
        & the stream threading lightly
        from silent Maro
   through the city in a whisper of spirits
      into the Triton's mouth.
But you go astray in this madness;
      you run from my eyes, not from Rome,
      and you think you will trip me up;
but your nets are laid badly,
      your scheme is transparent.
& I know you will feel

the ruin of your reputation
as much as you ought to;
It is nothing to me, personally,
that loose tongues abuse you,
that no good is spoken of you in all Rome.
One cannot, after all, trust gossip,
eternal enemy of loveliness;
and after all, you have not been caught
poisoning anyone,
the sun has brought no such crime to light;
and if you consume the long night
in dalliance
once in a while,
that small wickedness leaves me unwounded.
Helen betrayed father & country
in her amorous mutability,
& was brought back alive, no writ condemning her;
And Aphrodite herself
was borne down by Mars's violent love
& she is no less
a respectable luminary on Olympus;
and Paris once laid a goddess [30] among sheep
in full view of Ida's whole population,
hamadryads saw it, & sileni,
& the father of that dance; [31]
and you, Naiad, you gathered the fruit,
catching it as it fell,
in a hollow place on the mountain.
And after that swarm of disgraces
can anyone ask "Why is she rich?"
or "Who was the donor" & "Is his money respectable?"
Rome's cup spills over

[30] Oenone, nymph of Mount Ida. [31] Pan.

[130]

if in these days
    one girl abstains from the fashion.
Lesbia enjoyed these pleasures before Cynthia,
    & the second can no more be blamed than the first.
The man who cries out for the lean virtues of old Rome
    cries out that he is a newcomer here.
You could no more dry the streaming sea
    or take down the high stars
        than enforce virginity in Rome.
That was once the custom, in Saturn's reign
    before Deucalion's waters rolled through the world;
But after the flood receded, tell me
    who kept a chaste bed,
what goddess was content with one god only?
& don't forget Minos' gleaming queen
    with that bull,
    & Zeus, entering the brass donjon,
        nor could Danaë deny him.
If you would follow illustrious examples,
    the exemplary Greeks, the exemplary Romans,
    live in liberty then, with my understanding.

33

Now the cycling rites return;
    for ten nights now
        Cynthia has let the night bleed out
to mysteries engendered
        in the heat of the Nile.
The sacrament sent
        from the Lady of Egypt
            to the daughters of Rome
is most odious,
    inflicting hard abstinence
        on longing lovers.
You were always a bitter goddess, Io.
For your secret nights with Zeus
            you felt the dust
                of the world's roadways;
Hera crowned you with horns
        & you lost your girlish voice
            & the oak foliage wounded your mouth
and in your stall
    you shifted bitter leaves in your jaws.
Have you become disdainful
    now that you've become a proper deity?
Do Egypt's dark children
            please you no longer,
                must you come to distant Rome?
Does it please you
            for girls to sleep alone?
Watch out, wild goddess,
you may find the horns all anew,
    your ritual driven from these hills.
Nilotic cults are alien to the Tiber.
        And you, Cynthia, you enjoy my distress too much.

But come, after these starlit exemptions,
    let us triple our efforts.
But you notice my words
    only to smile at them.
Icarian oxen turn the stars slowly
    on their northern axle;
Phlegmatic, you continue to drink
      undaunted
        at midnight.
Doesn't your arm tire
    of throwing the anklebones?
God damn the man
    who first made wine from the grape
      & ruined good water with it.
The peasants of Attica
    who did in Icarius
      for making them drunk
were not altogether wrong,
    for the wine scent is bitter.
      Eurytion the centaur, & Polyphemus also,
would testify to that.
    Wine imperils glamour
      & gets the better of manhood,
& a woman in the heat of wine
    may forget her proper lover.

But . . . I speak too harshly,
    I don't mean it.
Bacchus cannot change you,
    so imbibe and look lovely;
the fruit of the vine
    becomes you.
Your trailing laurel hangs over the cup
    & my music

lifts your soft voice.
Let the wine drench the table
and foam from your golden chalice;
no woman withdraws
to her chamber alone
with pleasure;
Love always compels
a certain desire
for a certain one . . .
And the fires burn hotter
with absence;
It is too long abundance
that retards the flame.

34

Would any man
    entrust beauty he loves
        to the care of Cupid?
Through such naïveté
    was my mistress nearly removed
        from my affections.
The words proceed from experience;
    no friend is reliable in love
        and rarely will a man not try
to obtain what beauty he sees.
Eros sets kinsmen apart,
    sets one friend apart from another,
        brings men out of agreement into conflict.
Menelaus made his guest welcome,
        collected his pay as a cuckold,
    & Medea followed a stranger out of Colchis.
Now Lynceus, would you lay hands on Cynthia?
    Would shame not palsy your grip?
Good thing she's a girl fixed in her affections,[32]
    but if she weren't, could you live in such turpitude?
Strike out my life with steel or poison,
    take your choice,
    but desist from chasing this one girl.
May you be my lifelong friend,
    master of all my affairs,
    excluding affairs of the bedchamber;
I want no man (or god, for that matter) as a rival;
    My own light shadow raises suspicion,
    and I endure fear & trembling

[32] This line should dispel the long-held scholarly notion that Propertius lacked humor.

when there is no cause discernible
    but my own fool's passion.
But you broached those words
    while drunk,
  which is forgivable,
    for wine sets words awry,
but your mask of austerity will never fool me,
    for you know as well as the next man
    what a fine thing love is.
Now that you have at last lost your mind
    with this desire
  I delight only in your new allegiance
    to my lovelier deities.
What good do your Platonic platitudes
    do you now, and those weighty expositions
    of the nature of things?
What hope lies
    in your tuneful Greek plectrum?
Your ancient masters wrote no love manuals;
    better to attend the Muse of Philetas,
    & hearken to the dreams
    of modest Callimachus.
If you put to verse again
    how the course of the Aetolian river-god
    was broken,
& how the eddying Maeander loses itself
    in its own convolutions,
  or how Adrastus' horse Arion
pronounced the obsequies
    at the bleak burial of Archemorus,
It won't help you, having no bearing
    on your present situation,
nor will retelling how Amphiaraus' chariot
    fell into that hole,

or the story of Zeus's striking Capaneus to cinders.
Leave lofty noises to Aeschylus
    & quit unraveling your talent with the choros;
instead cut your verses on a narrower lathe
    & come sing in your own fire.
Homer was not immune to your ailment, nor Antimachus,
    for beauty sneers at godly greatness.
But no bull plows without apprenticeship
        on a noose,
    nor can you undergo grim love just yet;
        but let my song be your beginning.
No girl asks reasons
      for the way of the world
        or the course of the moon,
    or if a judge sits enthroned
        beyond the waters of hell,
    or if it is a god crackles the lightning.
Consider my condition: a small fortune,
        no generals among my forebears;
    yet I reign at the table
in the company of young women,
this being the product of those skills
        you take so lightly.
Though a man wounded
    (Eros' true aim has struck me down)
I have enough strength
   to relax among old wreaths.
I leave to Vergil such fields
    as Actium's coast watched over by the sun
        & that big fleet of Caesar's—
Vergil, who lifts up the Trojan sword again
    & recasts walls on the Lavinian coast.
Make way, you Roman writers, & you Greek writers,
    for the Iliad lies forgotten

& a greater work sees the light of day.
But Vergil, you also sing
 beneath the shadowing pines of Galaesus,
 & your reed flute polishes Daphnis' tune
  & the tune of ten apples
   & an unweaned goat given
to break a girl's resistance.[33]
And if Vergil tires of his oatstalk,
  the libertine dryads will still celebrate his name
   which can bring enchantment
   to the adages of Hesiod.
Speak of what field the wheat will stand in,
 what ridge the grape will fatten on;
You sing like Apollo ruling the turtle shell
 & the result will not go unnoticed
  or unthanked by your readers,
whatever their feelings
about my kind of poetry.[34]
Varro as well took up amorous verse,
   with weightier matters done,
    Varro being the great flame of Leucadia;
and love was wanton Catullus' tune,
   thus Lesbia is more renowned than Helen;
and love gave Calvus voice
  when he sang Quintilia's threnody;
and the late love-wounded Gallus spoke
   to the same measures;
And now
  if the gods let it be
   Propertius lifts up
 his exaltation of Cynthia
  among the great songs.

---

[33] At this point I have omitted a tiresome list of Vergilian stories.
[34] Two lines of the Latin, which compare Vergil and the poetaster Anser, have been omitted here.

BOOK III

1

Eidolon of Callimachus, & holy Philetas,
    I ask your sufferance,
      let me tread in your wood;
I come down, the first votary
          from the crystal fountain
      to weave Italian mysteries
         among the Greek dances.
Lift your voice, under what cliff
      did you thread your song?
What beat did you move to,
    what waters cleared your lips?
Let no one detain
    Apollo among weapons;
        let polished blades of verse be honed
      with the fine-grained pumice.
These songs will lift me up
      to a more exalted altitude;
my Muse rides victorious
        with flowered horses,
& the torches of Eros
        burn in my chariot;
a turmoil of dabblers in verse
         coming after.
Why do you give your horses their head
        in such useless contention?
No wide road ascends the mountain
      of the Muses.
Many will add honor to Roman annals;
       and some tout Bactra in Persia
as a fit imperial cornerpost;

But my pages bring
by undefiled path
    a book down from Parnassus
    that you may read in peace.
Pegasides, crown your poet with a delicate wreath,
      no hard diadem will do.
My good name
    now trod down
    will flower on my grave.
Dust fertilizes our reputation;
    our lips round out
    the names of the dead
      with greater reverence.
Who would know of the citadel
    brought down by the timber horse,
or of Hector befouled beneath the axle
    hauled three times around Troy's wall?
Priam's illustrious sons [1] would not be known
    in their own lands;
There would be little known of Ilion
    twice seized at the will
    of the Greek numen.
Homer himself, who recounted the ruin,
    has seen his work grow
    with running time.
I foresee that Rome will praise me
after the fire;
  my tombstone
    will not be disdained.
Apollo
  who hears my vows
    will see to it.

[1] The names of Priam's illustrious sons, given in the Latin, are omitted here, as is also an obscure allusion to Achilles.

2

Let us meanwhile
　　return to the ring of song,
　　　　let its usual pleasure touch her.
Orpheus allured feral beasts
　　　　with the Thracian lyre
　　　　　　and bewitched the rivers;
The singing lute strung mountain rocks
　　into a Theban wall [2]
and Polyphemus' song
　　wheeled about the foam-speckled horses
　　　　　of the sea-goddess Galatea
beneath the fires of Aetna.
Should we then stand amazed
　　　　that a crowd of maidens cherish our words,
　　we who are favored by Apollo
　　　　　& beloved of Bacchus?
My dwelling is simple,
　　its roof without gold,
　　　　without ivory vaults;
no black-marbled colonnade graces the porch,
　　I have no fields of fruit trees
　　　　nor fountains watered
　　　　　　by the Marcian aqueduct.
But I go
　　a companion of the Muses,
　　my verses are favored by those who read,
　　　　& Calliope does not tire
　　　　　　of my dancing tune;
My book celebrates
　　a fortunate woman,

2 See AMPHION in glossary.

My songs will be a monument to her beauty,
    for neither the rich pyramids
      lifted high beneath the stars
  nor Zeus's great sanctuary
        on the mountain of heaven
        nor the golden crypt of Mausolus
is spared death's final ravages.
    Fire and rain erode their greatness
      & they will be ruined & broken in,
But the name of genius is hewn
      in timeless glory,
the grace of genius eludes destruction.

3

In the mountain's soft shadow
  I stretched recumbent by springwater,
    Pegasus' spring on Helicon,
  thinking I would versify a tale
    of Alba's kings & royal works,
      thinking I had it in me,
& I set my lips to the great fountain
  where Ennius formerly drank,
    father Ennius, who sang the Curii,
      and the javelins of their adversaries;
who sang of the kingly plunder
  in the craft of Aemilius;
    who sang of Fabius Cunctator
      victorious,
    and sinister misfortune at Cannae,
      & of the gods hearing pious rogations
        & the Lares driving Hannibal
          from the sacred places;
and of the cry of the goose [3]
    so propitious for Rome.

But Apollo watched from the trees
    before a cave
  leaning on his golden cithara
    & said:
"Lunatic, who asked you to muddy
    the fountain?
Your glory lies elsewhere,
  so roll your small wheels
    on softer terrain.

---

[3] The outcry of geese in front of Jove's temple warned the Romans
of an attack by the Gauls.

Your book will be the lonely reading
        of a nervous girl awaiting her lover
    & will be put down at his arrival.
Propertius, why do your tunes
        revolve in wrong orbits?
Your skiff is fast and light,
        let your oars flash close to shore;
        avoid the trackless sea."
So spoke Phoebus Apollo, & with ivory plectrum
        he pointed out a footpath
                moss-grown on the forest floor
    and a sea-green cave
                studded with chrysoprase,
        tambourines hanging from the walls,
                from soft stone concavities.
& the mysteries of the Muses
                floated among the rocks,
        & a clay idol of father Silenus stood there,
        & there were reed panpipes,
                & Cytherean pigeons crowded their red beaks
                into the Hippocrene cistern
    & the nine delicate-fingered deities
                were about their work,
        winding ivy on the staff,
                measuring song to the lyre,
                lacing roses into wreaths,
    whereupon Calliope, the fiery beauty,
    touched me, & spoke:
"Be content to follow the path
                of the bright swan always;
        shun the road of the rattling cavalry,
                shiver no airs with brass-throated war note;
Keep the stain of war from the leaves of Helicon.
    The standards of Marius

stand without your help,
& you need not celebrate
Teutonic wars reddening the dismal Rhine,
clotting its waters with corpses.
You will sing instead
of the lover in laurel
waiting before his truelove's lintel,
you will sing the passwords
of drunken night flights,
and through your artful incantations
guarded girls may be sung loose
from their suspicious proprietors."
So said the goddess,
& she then baptized my lips
from the fountain of Philetas.

4

The Führer [4] considers
   invading the opulent East;
   slitting the jewelly waters
     of the Arabian Sea
      with his fleet,
the loot to be considerable,
      and the farthest earth will bear Rome's heel.
Tiber and Euphrates will both run beneath
     our bundle of sticks,[5]
& the Parthian trophies will shake under Zeus's artillery.
   Slide war-toughened prows into the sea
     & unfurl the canvas,
  conduct armed horses to their usual service
    and I will sing to your good luck.
Go and expiate
    the dishonor of that disaster of Crassus;
      Do well
      for our annals;
May father Mars & the fateful fires of holy Vesta
  grant
    that before my days run to a close
     I may see chariots returning,
        axles groaning with plunder,
and hear the cheers of the crowd
     as the horses pick through the throng.
And I will watch the procession,
     Cynthia's lap for a pillow,

---

[4] Propertius' phrase *deus Caesar* was not yet usual in Augustan poetry. In order to convey the nature of this piece and to clarify Propertius' attitude toward Augustus, I have been crude where the original was subtle, thus taking liberties with this not very good poem.

[5] The fasces, Roman symbol of authority.

& read out the list of cities seized,
    gaze at the javelins
of the vanquished cavalry,
    the bows of the trousered barbarians,
    and their captured chieftains
      sitting close by their stacked weapons,
all led by Caesar.
Let Venus aid her progeny; [6]
    Aeneas has yet his great descendants
    and the spoils of war go to those
      who labor to win them.
I am content to applaud on the Via Sacra.

[6] Venus' progeny are the Roman people, particularly the Julian line, of which Augustus was an adopted member. There is, however, a possible reference to Propertius himself as Venus' great poet.

5[7]

Love being a peaceable god
    we lovers venerate peace,
        & I struggle only with my mistress.
My soul doesn't ache for secret gold
        & attendant misfortunes,
    I don't slake my thirst
        from jeweled chalices,
and the fat Campania isn't burdened with my oxen,
    & I wield no shovel in Corinth
    looking for buried bronzes.
Primeval earth & contriving Prometheus
    were a ruinous combination;
and men were made
        with bodies more excellent than minds:
    Prometheus forgot the soul
        in his art:
that should have been shining perfection,
    flawless & true before all else.
Now we are wind-tossed on wide oceans;
    we go looking for trouble,
        and are always restocking our armories.
But treasure to the slough of Acheron?
    Most unlikely. You will ride
    the ship of hell, fool,
        with no shirt on your back.
The victor will come with the vanquished,
    Marius with Jugurtha; rich Croesus
        no less a shadow than the beggar Irus.
But the death most preferable comes
    after we have tasted the fruits of life;

[7] Nothing else in Propertius' work is quite like this unusual poem,
which should be read together with III.4.

And it is my delight to have worshiped Helicon
    from the beginning
      as a youth,
    and to have joined the Muses' dance.
Let it be my everlasting pleasure
    to lace my soul with wine
      spring roses wreathing my head;
and when the heaviness of years
    puts an end to love
      and white age dusts my black hair
    then vouchsafe certain pleasures;
To learn the nature of things,
    & what god governs this world;
      To understand mysteries;
      the waxing & waning of the moon,
    how the horns of the moon come
    to round out the month,
      where the winds come from
        whistling in the high seas;
    what the fluting east wind seeks for;
the source of the clouds' everlasting mists; I would know
if a day will come
    to bring down the towers of the world;
let it be my pleasure
    to learn why the red arc in the sky
      feeds on the rainwaters,
      why the earth moves under Mount Pindus;
why the sun's bright ring mourns
    with horses enshrouded in black;
& why Boötes delays in rolling the oxen & wagon;
why the Pleiad choros meets
    with close-set fires in the sky;
why deep oceans don't overrun their rims;
    and why the year fills with the four seasons.

Whether underground such things exist
    as the rule of gods,
      and if there are giants in torment there;
   whether black snakes twist Tisiphone's face;
       whether the Furies torture Alcmaeon
       & hungry Phineus.
If they exist there, the wheel, the sliding boulder,
      and thirst in the running stream;
   If triple-headed Cerberus guards the mouth of hell,
      & if Tityos is bound to his 9 acres;
Or if these stories brought down to us
    are mere fiction
    and there is nothing to fear
      after the final fire.
This is the remainder of my life,
    that which awaits me.
And you, pleased so much by war,
      bring back the standards of Crassus.

6

Tell me, Lygdamus,
    what you have observed
        of your mistress and mine.
And without lies,
    and your yoke might thereby be lifted.
You wouldn't buoy my spirits
        with empty gladness,
    you wouldn't deceive me,
        bringing back news you suspect I would like to believe?
No envoy should come
    bearing empty words,
      and a slave should be truthful
      if only out of fear.
Now, begin at the beginning,
    if you remember anything;
      I will take it all in with eager, doubtful ears.[8]
You saw her cry, thus, with unkempt hair,
  a great quantity of water spilling from her eyes, Lygdamus?
& you beheld
    a mirror thrown down on the couch,
      & the jewels no longer adorning
        her lovely fingers;
Did a sad gown drape her delicate shoulder,
    did her jewel box lie closed
      at the couch-foot?
And you say the house was dreary? and the maids
    sad at the loom, Cynthia not gone
      from among them?
Did she dry her eyes with the wool,
    & bring up my complaints in a shrill voice,

---

[8] The reading "eager, doubtful ears" is a plausible translation of the Latin, given the context.

"Is this his promised reward for me—
        the promise you witnessed, Lygdamus?
    & Lygdamus, a slave who lies is in trouble.
Can he abandon me,
    leave me miserable for no good reason,
        & now keep housed the sort of woman
            I prefer not to speak of?
He delights that I shrivel up in my bed
            without company.
If it would please him, let him dance at my funeral.
It is by no talent
            the bitch has beaten me,
    but by love-philters, by potions;
he is brought to her by the rhombos
            circling on its string,
and by awful swollen bramble toads,
    and the bones she has cut out of snakes,
        and screech owl plumes got from low-lying tombs,
and the wool riband wound
            around his effigy.
But unless my dreams sing portending nothing,
        his pain will be late, but sufficient
            at my feet.
The spider will foully web
        his empty bed,
    and in their nights together
        may Aphrodite herself lie elsewhere."

If these lamentations
came from a true soul,
            Lygdamus,
        then run the path back
        and by my mandate report
        that I may have been angry

in my tears, but never false,
   that I am turned in a similar fire,
and that for a week and a half I have lain *completely* pure.
If, by some chance,
      you bring about a joyful reunion, then—
         insofar as I can help—
you will be a free man, Lygdamus.

7

Hot pursuit of gain
etches worry into the brow,
    leads down a steep road
        to a premature end;
wealth the seed of our rising inquietude,
           feeder of vice. In that service
my friend Paetus set linen to wind, toward Alexandria
        in the usual treasure hunt,
          and was buried in the surge of the windy sea;
The fortune he sailed for
        left him bereft of youth and life,
and he floats in a distant gulf
      nibbled on by curious fish,
and his mother can't bury him with the proper ritual
   or plant his corpse among kinsmen.
Now the seabirds float over his bones,
        his tomb the liquid Carpathian.
His life was a trifling plunder
        for the sea's doyens. Why,
         Neptune, did you fracture that keel?
And other good men sank in the sea
         with that hollow ship
   as well.
And he pled his youth,
      pled a bereaved mother,
  bootless cries in the choking sea,
    for the waves have no attentive gods.
His ship was moored fast to the rocks
      but the night storm struck
the hawsers through
  and swept ship and crew away.
Gods, give his body back, at least, to dry land;

[154]

His life is lost in silent sea-depths.
Let him lie sand-drifted
and when a seafarer sails by his grave
let him say that brave men
might well fear death by water.
Go build curved keels,
weave the sails of death;
men's hands have wrought such ruin at sea.
Earth being too small a tomb
we add the ocean,
by artifice we lengthen
the evil path of fortune.
Can an anchor hold a man
whose household gods cannot?
What shall a man merit
whose homeland is too small?
What he builds is at the wind's mercy,
for rarely does a hull get old and rot,
and you can't count on a safe harbor.
Cruel Nature put the sea
at the disposal of avarice and ambition
usually unrealized.
A wild coast testifies to Agamemnon's grief,
where the pain of Argynnus
brands the waters below the mountain.
For a drowned youth
the Greek ships did not weigh anchor;
Iphigenia killed for the delay.
And rocks broke the triumphant fleet,
Greece thus shipwrecked and sea-ravaged.
A few at a time Ulysses mourned them, his friends,
his wit worthless against the ocean waves.
Had Paetus contented himself
with cultivating his fields

and his patrimony,
he would still enjoy the boisterous banquet
in the warmth of his hearth-gods,
a pauper, but a dry one.
Poverty would then be a minor complaint.
He was not cut out for for the scream of sea squalls,
and his hands were burnt by the rope;
The marbled bedchamber & well-pillowed terebinth couch
were more his style.
But the running sea
tore his nails at the last;
A hard night saw him drifting by ship's timber;
many evils convened that he might perish.
He wept and cried out,
black brine closing around him:
"Aegean gods, water rulers,
Lords of the wind and waves washing over me,
where have my best years gone?
Did I sail these narrows
crime staining my hands?
I am driven against cliffs,
I am struck with the trident.
Let the surf float me up
on an Italian beach
that my mother may bury me."
The churning water took him then,
the last words and days for him.
Nereus' hundred daughters, born of the sea,
might have helped him,
and Thetis, who knew a mother's grief once.
And as for me,
the north wind shall never ravel my sails,
and I will remain here where I belong
at the portals of my mistress.

8

It was a most delightful melee
    we enjoyed last night under lantern light
when with choked cries of rage
      & multiple maledictions
      & reeling in the heat of wine
you shoved over the table
         and flung the glassware at my head.
Come on,
   go after my hair with gusto
      & lunge at my face with your pretty claws,
swear to burn out my eyes with a close-held flame
     & rip the toga from my shoulders;
For it proves a true fire of love.
No woman free of Eros' hammerlock
      cries out in such manner.
She who rails with an angry tongue
     does so groveling at Aphrodite's feet.
And she plays hard to get,
     hiding in a swarm of chaperones;
  or else she dances drunk in the street
    to the bacchanalian dithyrambs;
     & black phobic nightmares come to her each night.
A girl's portrait
      decorating a tablet
    is an apparition moving her to misery.
It takes no diviner
    to detect true love in this turmoil;
If it can't be fired to anger, love has no fidelity.
    Let my enemies
enjoy maidens of cold disposition.
Notice the marks of her teeth in my neck;
  let bruises tender evidence

that I have enjoyed her company;
I wish for contention in love, to hear cries
       & to see tears, whether mine or yours,
but I abhor secret words in your eyes
       & silent signals sent with your fingers.
I hate those heaving sighs in the night
      that never break through sleep;
I should always wish to have a woman of spirit.
The flame was sweeter to Paris
      after he broke through Greek swords
         to bring its fiery pleasure
           to Helen, Tyndareus' daughter.
While the Greeks gained victory
      & as rocklike Hector savagely withstood assault
         Paris fought the greater war
rolling & struggling with his mistress.
I will always contend either with you
        or for you, with my competition,
& I ask for no peace.

   . . . .

Dance for joy, that no woman is as beautiful as you are; [9]
   you would grieve if one were,
      but still, it is suitable for you to be proud.
But to him, snare setter
  who would capture the pleasures
of our bed,
May his father-in-law
     last a century,
& his mother-in-law
      come to live with him.
If he has tasted the fruit
  of the fire

[9] These final sixteen lines are usually treated as a separate poem.

in a stolen night,
    it was through her craving
      to offend me;
She did not love him.

9

My lord Maecenas,
  come down from Tuscan kingly blood,
the groove of your fortune is clear enough,
so why, why would you have me engrave
        songs in the sea,
  & bend a thin mast with overspread sails?
It is most inglorious
      to take up a heavy pack
          only to break beneath it
and then run for cover;
No man is suitable for all things,
    the flame is not brought down
          from every hill.
      .   .   .   .

Some whip their teams for the prize at Olympia
    & some are born with the glory of speed afoot;
Some men are sown for peace
    & some men are raised for the armed camp;
the seed grows by its particular nature.
But Maecenas, having received the precepts
      that govern your life,
          I will go past your example.
Your glorious axes could fall in the Forum,
        your law handed down there;
You could, if you wished,
      beat down the pikes
          of the quarrel-prone Medians
        & nail enough trophies to your walls
            that they would creak with the weight.
Though great Caesar gives you the power
        to do what you will,
        and wealth insinuates its way

into your coffers
at all seasons,
you still keep back, and live in shadows,
without ostentation;
you draw in the overstretched sails.
But believe me when I say
your name will equal Camillus' in men's judgment;
and your name will be on men's lips,
and your footfall will be heard in glory
close behind Caesar;
Good faith will be your true monument.
I, however, will not cut through distended waves
in a boat under full sail;
I remain in the backwash.
  I will not spill out again the tearful story
of the towers of Cadmus incinerated by father Zeus,[10]
or of 7 battles equally disastrous.
Nor will I again recount
the story of the Scaean gate & Pergama,
Apollo's rampart,
nor the return of the Danaän ships for the tenth spring,
when the Greeks plowed under Neptune's walls,
after that Palladian stratagem with the timber horse.
It is rather my joy
to have won a place among the books of Callimachus
& to have sung
to Philetas' Doric measures.
Let my scribbling
set a fire
under young men and under young women;

---

[10] The Latin here may refer to the destruction of the walls of Thebes
by the Epigoni, as W. A. Camps has it, or to the incineration of Semele
and the palace of Cadmus when Zeus appeared to her in full glory. I
have chosen the latter interpretation.

Let *them* cry my deification,
    & bear sacrifice to my altar.
But,[11]
      with you as my general,
        I will sing Jupiter's artillery,
      and the giants menacing heaven;
    and I will sing the 2 kings fattened
        at the teats of the forest wolf.
I will lay out the warp of walls shored up
        at Remus' killing,
    & I will weave bulls through the high Roman hills;
My genius will inflate itself
      at the drop of a word.
I will attend your chariots
        singing hallelujahs
    from one rim of the world to the other;
I will sing how the Parthians dropped their lances.
      in astute retreat;
    & the camps on the Nile broken through
        by Roman iron,
      & Antony done in by his own hand.
Merely
    grasp the reins
        of the new course undertaken,
    and give me an auspicious banner
    as my wheels roll forth;
This is your laudable concession, Maecenas,
    and it is your due
    that men should call me
      one of your company.

---

[11] I have translated the excesses of the final section of the poem as sarcasm, and if the tribute to Maecenas at the beginning is honest, as I believe it is, then this treatment is tenable by assuming that the final section is a protest against what Maecenas would have the poet write, not a complaint about Maecenas himself.

10

In the red-lit dawn
    I beheld with wonder
        Muses at the couch-foot,
And the omen they brought
    of a most special birthday
        echoed in the morning;
So let it be
    a day without clouds
        and the sky without winds,
a day in which the waves slide gently
        onto dry beaches,
    and one in which
        I see no grieving
            in the day's light.
Let marble Niobe suppress
    that glissade of tears
and the complaints of the kingfisher fall
        silent on sea dune
    and Itys' mother have respite from wailing.
May my dearest mistress
        so auspiciously descended
    rise up now and supplicate
        the prayer-demanding gods,
and first dispel the night's sleep
        with clear water
    and arrange that shining hair,
And next, Cynthia, put on those silks
    that so captivated Propertius,
        caught his eye,
& make sure your hair
    doesn't lack for flowers
        and entreat the gods that the beauty

which is your strength
    be everlasting.
May you always be
    sovereign queen of my affections.
When you have burned incense
    before the crowned altars
      and the flame has glittered
through the whole house
    with sanctification,
Let there then be consideration of a banquet
    where the light will run out until morning
      among the wine cups.
Anoint yourself with saffron & myrrh from onyx cask
    & let us dance to the shinbone flute
      until the hoarse tune fails;
Indulge yourself
    in light words
    & may the cheer of the feast
      keep off unwelcome sleep
& the nearby roads ring with reveling.
    Let there be dice thrown
    the rattling bones determining
      who will be flogged by Eros' wing feathers
and after the wine is consumed
    and the exact hour comes
when Aphrodite prepares
    the sacred ministrations
    Let us fulfill the year's rite
      in our bed
    & thus complete the commemoration.

11

Will you be amazed
    that a woman can twist my life,
        bend virility to her desire?
Your mocking lacks decency;
    no shame lies in lacking means
        to shatter the yoke,
          to fracture the chain.
It is not a matter of cowardice.
There is no better forecast of a fatal sea
    than a sailor's intuition;
    the bite of the blade teaches soldiers fear,
        and I sing a new tune, now,
          my youth gone,
and you might well walk fearfully
        after my example.
Enchanting Medea set fiery bulls into action
under a steel yoke,
    & planted the clash of iron
        in the sword-bearing earth,
    closed the great jaws
        of the guardian reptile
        so the golden wool might go to Aeson's house.
And the fierce queen of Amazons [12]
        rattled arrows among the Greek ships
        from horseback;
& she conquered her conqueror,
    with the radiance of loveliness laid bare,
        splendor under golden armor.
And Hercules, who raised the pillars
    of a world pacified,
took down a day's worth of weaving

[12] The queen of the Amazons was Penthesilea, slain by Achilles at Troy.

in Omphale's service—such was the glory
    of her beauty, she who was once lacquered
      by Gygaean lakewater.
Semiramis, mistress of Babylon,
    erected ramparts,
      brick upon brick,
ample for two chariots passing
    neither axletree clipping the other;
She ran the Euphrates among her towers
    & ruled above Bactra's genuflections.
And there is the example of gods
  and the example of heroes.
    Zeus himself
    is disgraced in his own house.
And remember the affair of that woman
  who lately tainted our swords with shame,
    who took her salacious leave
even among servants. Whose fee,
    from her foul suitor,
      was the battlements of Rome
    & a senate under her dominion.
The dust of Alexandria spawns artifice,
    Egypt's bloody crimes stain Memphis,
      where the sand absorbed Pompey's triple conquests.
No coming day will blot out this infamy;
    better, Pompey, had you died,
      ill that time in Naples,
    or bent your head to your father-in-law.
Slattern queen, the stain of Ptolemy on her,
    queen of whores under the skies of Egypt
she would have Anubis bay at Jupiter,
    drown out the bugle with the jingle of sistrum,
& slide past the Roman prow
      with a poled barge,

& unfurl the mosquito net as her canopy
        on the Capitoline,
hand down law among Marian monuments & arms.
And Rome, ruling the world from 7 hills,
       cringed at a woman's power.
What good would it be
     that we crumpled the axes of arrogant Tarquin
     only to now endure a queen?
But she retreated to her twisting Nile in fear,
   and her wrists knew our chains;
Rome saw her arms under the hollow teeth
      of sacred snakes,
  & by secret arteries
      her limbs drew in dreams.
"Why did you cower, O Rome?" she said, "for one of your
     citizens was a man."
Her voice thus, from the wine fumes.

11*a*[13]

But now, unshaken Rome,
  pray for a long day for Augustus.
Curtius went into the cleft,
     founding his monument thereby,
& Decius broke battles from horseback,
  & Horatio's footpath still testifies to that bridge cutting.
The gods threw these walls up,
    & while Caesar retains his health
       Rome need fear nothing from heaven.
Where now are Scipio's warships, or Camillus' standards,
     or Mithridates', lately seized by Pompey's fist,
& where is Hannibal's loot, & the trophies
    of Syphax beaten?
And Pyrrhus' glitter is ground in the dirt underfoot.
Apollo will bring to mind again
    the sharp edge of armies broken,
  & the one day of war that did so much;
and the sailor must now be mindful of Caesar,
      in port or outward bound;
even the sea
   being his domain.

---

[13] This poem is usually considered part of III.11. The original text is confused, but I follow H. E. Butler's transpositions and continue from *Curtius expletis* with a new poem in order to save III.11 from complete disintegration.

12

Postumus, can you leave her, tears in her face,
                              Galla your wife,
    & follow the soldier's trade,
                    behind Caesar's flags?
What good is Parthian plunder,
                your wife's prayerful cry unheeded?
If the law allows it,
      let them all be damned equally,
          who go abroad looking for gold,
   along with any man who prefers
      the arms of the camp
         to those awaiting him in his bed,
You must be unhinged,
    to drink from distant rivers
      at day's end,
  helmet for a bucket, mantle thrown over your arm,
    while she, meanwhile,
    will toss in her bed with each hollow rumor,
    afraid your manly valor
      will bring you to a bitter end;
afraid the Median arrows will sing
             at your riddled death,
  or that you will fall by iron
    at the hand of some cataphract
      on a gold-trimmed horse;
afraid you will be brought back in a jar,
      something to cry over;
         and that is how they bring them home.
You are several times blessed, Postumus,
    in such a chaste bride;
      your custom is somewhat unworthy of her.
Think what she might do here, unshackled from respectable
                                    fear,

her husband gone, with all Rome
instructing her in dissipation.
But you have nothing to worry about,
her bed will never be for sale;
and she won't dwell on your harshness.
And when fate remits you safe & sound
Galla will embrace you
with no crime to blush for.
And Postumus will seem
to a wondering audience
another Ulysses—at least in his choice of wives.
Ulysses, after all,
was undamaged by his delay, a 10-year campaign
from Ismara to Gibraltar, overcoming all obstacles:
Circe's alluring cunning, the Cyclops' den, the binding lotus
weed,
the waters rumbling from Scylla to Charybdis & back
again,
incautious hunger, tearful Calypso's chamber,
a long cold swim, the black hall of noiseless
shadows,
the siren's sea
got past with deaf men at the rowing bench;
and he renovated an ancient bow
to the ruin of a number of suitors;
at which point his vagrancy ended—
and he came home safe, & not in vain,
for his wife retained
her honor
& his.
But Aelia Galla,
if necessary,
would surpass that record
of marathon chastity.

13

Women's desires endear the night,
   Rome's ruined fortune being Aphrodite's doing;
This rioting luxuriance
                  cedes these evils.
Gold out of India,
        nautilus from the eastern seas,
            purple from Tyre,
Bedouin cinnamon brought camelback
                out of Arabia;
These are weapons in the wars of love,
    And they seduce chaste girls
        shut up in their rooms,
even those girls disdainful as Penelope.
   Matrons walk abroad
          wearing the goods of spendthrifts
          & linger before our eyes
             with the booty of harlotry.
There is no reverence, no reluctance in asking or giving,
     or if there is
          the delay is removed at a price.

Oriental burials display more honor
        when the red dawn lights the husband's pyre
         & the bier receives the last torch;
Then the commotion of wives with outspread hair begins,
    wives devoted enough to struggle with one another
        to follow their husbands
and escape the disgrace of widowhood,
    burning lip and breast against the dead.
Here, adultery only;
no woman in Rome sleeps with
    Evadne's fidelity

or Penelope's constancy.
It was better in the old days
    when our peaceful riches lay
        in crop & orchard.
Our forebears shook down apples
    & gave them as offerings,
      & fat baskets dark with blackberries,
  picked violets & lilies, offered grapes
    & glossy-feathered birds.
With these small seductions
      girls surrendered kisses to their lovers
    in secluded declivities and groves,
a deerskin the only blanket over them,
    and the tall grass would make a bed,
        pine trees spreading slow shadows on the
          ground around them.
Nor did pain attend the sight of godly nakedness.
The horned lead ram himself
      would restore the fat sheep
    to the deserted court
      of the great god of the forest.
And the gods of the fields
     spoke soft words to men
    before their hearths
and the god Pan was patron
    of hunters
of rabbit and bird
    under the cliff.
But now the forest altars are abandoned,
  gold blinding men to duty.
Money erodes faith;
    the law itself is bought
      & justice lucre-bound,
  no law but the grasping hand

[172]

& impiety.
Seared entrance posts witness the sacrilege of Brennus,
Gaul who would have plundered
the oracle at Delphi;
Lightning glittered and the laurel-topped mountain shook
and Gallic spears were buried
in a winter storm.
The foul murder of Polydorus by his faithless kinsman
was due to the lure of gold.
And so that the gold-glint might be seen
on her smooth-muscled neck,
Eriphyle betrayed her husband
who was taken by the earth, he and his horses both.
Rome is crushed by luxury;
goods overwhelm her.
But no one believes it, having only my word for it.
The Trojans believed Cassandra less
when she foretold ruin,
saw alone
what Paris brought them,
the armed horse
inside the walls
by treachery.
But her madness served its purpose,
and her unbelieved words
lent final credence
to the gods.

14[14]

O Sparta of outlandish laws, outlandish custom,
how I envy your virginal gymnasia,
where naked girls enjoy the fun,
the wrestling,
retrieve stray balls, run
to the song of hoopstick & hoop.
Girls stand dust-drifted
at the race's end goal
& in Sparta a girl may join the pancration
giving & receiving her share,
glove tight on delighted fist.
She wheels in a circle
against the weight of the discus
& a maiden may be seen
running her father's dogs
in the long mountains of Taygetus
her hair gleaming with hoarfrost.
The Spartan girl
dances her horse in the ring
& buckles a sword to a white thigh
& hides her hair in hollow bronze,
stripped to the waist like a warlike Amazon
bathing in the Thermodon,
or like Helen taking arms
with bare torso
& shameless complexion
among her brothers,[15] the god Castor the horseman
& Pollux the boxer.
The law of Lacedaemon forbids

---

[14] This poem is an interesting sexual fantasy.
[15] Propertius seems to have invented this tale about Helen.

lovers to go separate ways
and you may be seen in the crossroads
with your girlfriend,
nor is any young woman
kept shackled up and guarded,
nor need any man fear the vengeance
of some sour cuckold.
You need no go-between
& you don't have to cool your heels
in the anteroom.
No crimson tunic deceives the inquiring glance
& no woman relies on scented hair.
But in Rome
women walk surrounded by custodians,
the way narrow,
not a finger insertable,
& you cannot find out
how you should look, or what you should say;
the lover travels an unlit path.
O Rome, if you would replicate
the Spartan customs
& take up their style of wrestling
you would be much the dearer to me.

15

These words
    that no storm break
      over this love,
That I not lie
    awake nightly without you—
When I veiled my boyhood modesty
    with the robe of manhood [16]
      & was set loose on amorous paths,
It was Lycinna tinged my soul
    those first nights,
      oiled that roughness.
And it was free.
But it has been three years,
    & since then maybe ten words
    have passed between us.
Your love buries my past;
    no woman since
      has sweetened her chain
      around my neck.[17]

. . . .

Now cruel Dirce swore to it
    that Antiope had lain with Lycus,
      & this "crime" so aroused Queen Dirce
    that she had Antiope's lovely hair singed,
    and she clawed her cheeks,
and freighted her unjustly
    with excessive labor at the loom,
and gave her a floor tile for a pillow
    and a black sty to live in,
and mocked hunger with water.

[16] The *toga virilis*.
[17] Some verses are missing in the Latin after this line.

Zeus, would you allow such a thing,
> wrist-cracking chains
>> for this young woman of yours,
>>> no aid in her bind?
But Antiope, with her own body's strength,
> cracked manacles from her hands,
>> then ran timidly to Cithaeron, mountain stronghold,
>>> night all around her, a sharp bed in thin hoarfrost,
>>>> fear at her elbow, with the noise of vagrant streams
(she feared her mistress following).
And she came then to her sons,
> but Zethus was not much upset
>> at his mother's misfortune,
& Amphion turned merely lachrymose.
But as silence settles after the east wind
> whirls against south wind,
>> and the sound of the sand grows thin
>>> on silent beaches,
> so her knees slid to earth;
>> & filial piety returns before bent knees.
(The old man that guarded these godly sons
> was worthy of Zeus their father.)
And as dutiful squires
> of their mother's honor
>> they dutifully avenged her,
strapping Dirce beneath a bull
> for a bloody death through the fields;
This for the glory of their mother;
> and Amphion sang
>> a paean of victory
>>> against the cliffs.
> But excuse my digression,
Cynthia,
> and excuse Lycinna

who has done you no wrong,
     even though it is painful for you
     to suppress your anger.
Let no talk stir
     of you and me;
I hope I may love you
     until the last fire
          settles in its ashes.

16

With midnight, my mistress's letter
    declaring I should come,
        forgoing delay, to Tibur
where doubled turrets float
    over white rock cliffs
        and the waters of Anio fall
in spreading pools.
With her mandate, indecision.
  In the night's veil
audacious hands might lay hold of my arms,
  but if I should delay, not come as she asks,
      her tears would be more fearful
than thieves cloaked in the dark.
    I sinned once before
      & paid a year's penance, repelled from her bed,
and those sharp and ready claws of hers
      are something to consider.
But no man would injure a lover,
    lovers being sacred;
Lovers can walk the road of the robber's nest,
    Sciron's road, and even the sands of Scythia
      molested by no man,
no man would wish to be so much a barbarian.
The moon glows over the road
  & the stars light the ruts therein
    & Eros the god himself
flames ahead with a blazing torch;
Even the wide-slung jaws
      of the mad dogs of the highway
are turned aside.
For lovers the road is safe at late hours—
  there is no profit in scattering their blood

and Aphrodite protects them.
But—
  should my undoing come
    & she perform the proper rites
    my death might be atoned for;
the price is worth it.
  She will bring incense to the fire
    & adorn my sepulcher with a crown of flowers.
She will bow in a vigil
    hard by my tomb.
May the gods grant that she not bury these bones
    in a tumultuous place
      near the congregation of the road;
    in such places are the tombs of lovers defiled.
Bury me in remote ground
    in the shadow of a leafy tree,
      or on a wild beach
        under a sand heap.
I do not want
    my name found in the common highway.

17

My rogation to Bacchus, before his altar:
   Give me peace, & an auspicious wind
        fattening my sails.
Your wine heals pain
   & you can overcome violent Love's
        present disdain;
For lovers are united by Bacchus
      & also released from love,
   and for his part,
       the god is not himself a novice,
        this attested to by Ariadne in the heavens
carried there by his lynxes.
O drown this pain in my soul,
    for only wine or death
      will numb the torment,
a slow fire locked in my bones.
A sober night is always agony
    for lonely lovers,
    hope and fear alternately shearing their souls,
but if Bacchus brings sleep to my bones
     through his gift,
      the hot flush of wine,
   then I will plant vines;
  cleat rows of vines to the hills
    & by vigilance assure
    that they are not ravaged by wild beasts.
If I may fill my vat with wine-dark must
     & tint my ankles with the new grape's dye,
then I will live my allotted years
    in the god's abundance,
  & I will be known as the poet of his virtues,
& I will proclaim his creation
     by the zigzag flame of Zeus,

& sing how his dancers conquered the soldiers of India,
  How Lycurgus went mad to no purpose
    with the new-brought drink,
How the 3 troops of maenads reveled
    in the doing-in of Pentheus,
& how the Tyrrhenian sailors turned into curved dolphins
    & slid overboard
      into the sea
        from the vine-knotted ship,
How his streams ran sweet through Naxos,
    streams from which the people there
      drank his liquor.
And, with his white neck bent
    for the slackened ivy clusters,
      the god's hair will be wreathed
        with a Lydian turban,
his smooth neck smeared
    with scented olive,
      loose robe brushing naked feet.
Dircean Thebes will beat the quiet timbrels,
  and goat-footed satyrs will play the reed pipe,
    the cymbals will beat out the harsh Idaean dance
  close by great Cybele,
      turret-crowned goddess.
Before the temple
    with the wine bowl
the high priest will decant the wine
    in a gold goblet
      over the offering.
I will repeat these things,
    sing of them
    not abjectly
    but with Pindaric cadence,
  only free me from these iron chains
    & break through my mind's turmoil with sleep.

18

Where the sea is closed out
    from the shadows of hell,
        breakers playing on the warm pools
            at Baiae,
Where Misenus, Trojan trumpet player, lies sand-buried,
        & Hercules' causeway booms in the ocean,
        & where the cymbals rang for the Theban god
        when he went auspiciously searching
            through mortal cities;
That place is now hateful,
            stained with black crime.
Baiae, what inimical god
        has stood forth in your waters?
Here Marcellus sank [18]
        to darker waves in Avernus;
his spirit moves vaguely
            among those pools.
What good did his bloodline
        or his highly placed mother do him,
        or his esteem at Caesar's fireplace?
Or the curtains floating
            over the crowds at the theater,
        & all the fine things his mother got him?
His sun has set
    in his 20th year;
his fortune swung on a short tether.
But go now,
        revive your spirit,
& pretend to the old triumphs,

[18] Marcellus died suddenly at Baiae; the imagery suggests drowning,
although he is not known to have died from that cause. He may have
been poisoned.

when the whole theater stood in applause;
Outfit yourself with gold again,
   & let the great games glitter again with jewels;
      for you will bring all this to the fire,
   & all men come to the fire,
      great lords equally
         with the wretched of the earth.
Terror lingers on the road,
   but every man's heel
      will rub that path.
All must come beg
   to the tune of the triple howl
      of the hound of Erebus;
All men must embark in the common boat,
   a grim & ancient man for oarsman.
Though a man look for security
      in iron & brass
      Death will yet take him by the hair
      & reave him from his hole.
Nireus went unexempted by splendid looks;
   Achilles went
      despite his muscle;
and no stream-borne gold saved Croesus.
But Charon, O pilot of pious ghosts,
   carry his spirit as men took his corpse;
Let his soul float on the sidereal ribbon
   far from the haunts of humans, where Caesar went,
& Claudius, who ruled the ground of Sicily.

19

You review our sins, declare man's soul is lust,
    but listen, when the flame breaks through a woman,
when you sunder the shackles of modesty,
       there is no measure to your frenzy.
A blaze in a wheat field might sooner be put out,
     or streams slide into their springs
      or the bleak shoals of the Syrtes allow refuge
      or the wild Malean coast welcome sailors,
than anyone hold you back in your desire
     or break the thrust of your unmastered passion.
Pasiphaë is my witness, who
        galled by the Minoan bull's disdain
           wore fir-wood horns that she might have him;
      & Tyro, glowing for Enipeus, wishing to lie
        with the watery god;
and Myrrha, changed to a leafy myrtle
     because she burned for her father.
Why should I have to speak of Medea, killer of children
      in her desire?
  Or of Clytemnestra, who darkened a kingdom
        with her crime,
     or of Scylla, who sold herself for
     a well-built Cretan—
Scylla whose razor to her father's hair
      cut down his realm;
         this was the dowry she promised Minos;
      such was the stealthy love
        that opened the king's gates;
And her reward
was to be dragged in the sea
    from the stern
      of the leaving ship.

Even so
    Minos deserves to be judge of the dead
        for he was a conqueror
        fair in his victory.
And you unmarried girls,
    may your pitch-pine wedding torches
        burn more auspiciously
      & with more moderation.

BOOK III

20[19]

Do you really think
    he gives a damn
        for your lovely figure?
You yourself saw
    how he abandoned your bed,
        a flint-souled man loving gold before beauty,
      & setting his sails accordingly.
But could all Africa be worth such a clamor?
And you,
    lacking good sense,
        keep rearranging his hollow words
        & and his empty oaths.
But now, perhaps,
another heart beats time
        against his own.
However,
    Your beauty is still potent,
       your Palladian talents are yet in order,
        and the great light of your learned forebear [20]
        shines in your eyes.
With a faithful lover
    your fortune will be sufficient,
      & there is a key to that treasure
        in my bedroom,
    if I may suggest it.

· · · · · · · · · · · · · · · · ·

The first night arrives.
    give us sufficient time

[19] It is possible that III.20 is really two poems, the second beginning
with line 26. In any event I believe that the woman referred to is
Cynthia, although W. A. Camps, on very slight evidence, argues other-
wise.
[20] Cynthia (Hostia) probably claimed descent from the poet Hostius.

in this great night;
Luna, let this first night
    be couched in your lingering
        splendor
and you, Phoebus, prolonging the downpour
    of the summer fires,
        shorten the road of your loitering flame.
But first the covenant must be made,
    the rules inscribed,
        the law written, in our new affair.
And Eros himself, with his own seal,
    binds fast the pact;
        the twisted sidereal diadem is witness.
Ah, how many hours
    must this discourse turn through
    before the goddess Aphrodite
        spurs us into lovely arms.
When the bed is not bound
    by true agreement
    then no avenging gods walk in the wakeful night,
    and violent desire
        will break the chain it forged;
But may initial good omens
    run continuous
        through a true love.
Therefore, whoever breaks
    our sacred contract,
        bound at the altar,
    whoever pollutes our mingled love
with outside embellishment,
Let all the pains known to love
    (& customary in it)
        then be his;
Let his privacy disappear

in the gossipy streets of Rome;
May that beloved window be
closed to him all night
despite all weeping.
Let him love forever
but be forever destitute
of love's fruition.

21

To break this hard passion
  I must make the great journey,
    Take the long road
      to erudite Athens,
And perhaps the flame
    constantly arising
      as I gaze at her raptly
        will then subside.
The fire feeds on itself and grows;
    I have tried all the patent medicines,
      but desire stays lodged in my heart,
  Eros oppresses me.
Her invitations are now few, refusals frequent,
    & when she condescends to lie with me
      she sleeps on the far edge of the bed,
        in her clothes.
One remedy remains: to leave,
      to shift my ground.
The road that removes me from her sight
      may remove her from my heart.
Come now, my fellow wayfarers,
      pull the ship into the sea,
    draw lots for oar duty,
    draw the auspicious sail to mast top
      & weigh anchor
  when the overslung sky
      favors the course of mariners
        on the glassy sea.
Farewell my friends,
    and farewell to the proud walls of Rome,
    & good-bye my beloved
      for what you were to me.

I will now be floated through rumbling breakers
        to the tune of my prayers to the sea-roaring gods
        through the Ionian Sea to the calm port of Lechaeum,
& the sails will be hauled down
        the small ship's mast.
From there, where the Corinthian isthmus
        cleaves the two seas,
I will foot the remainder of the road
        to Piraeus
        & I will mount the ramp of Theseus,
        slanting through the long walls up to Athens.
In Plato's school and Epicurus' garden
        I may begin to enlarge my wisdom
        & reap learned Menander's fruit,
& I will undertake rhetoric, the sword of Demosthenes.
        Of course I will take in the great paintings
        & please my eyes with the bronzework & the ivory.
Either the interval of years, or the long seas rolling between
        us,
        shall erase the scar in my heart;
If I die, it will be fate's work, not Aphrodite's,
        & I will not die in dishonor.

22

Has unheated Cyzicus
            agreed with you, Tullus,
      over these multiplying years;
      are you pleased with the sea's stir
            in the Propontis,
      and Cybele's beauty carved
            in the ivory tusk there,[21]
            and the road of the reaving god's horses,
            Pluto's road?
However much Helle's towers delight you
      may my hope for your return
            yet move you.
Should travel bring you
      to the sight of Atlas
      under the weight of all heaven,
      or the snaky Gorgon's corpse,
            or Geryon's stalls,
      or the scars in the powder of Libya
            where Hercules and Antaeus fought,
      or to the Hesperidean choros;
Should your oarsmen plash you past
            Colchian Phasis, & your ship's boards
      follow those of the Argo
            whose strange pine-form prow
      floated between cliffs under the flight of the dove;
Though you look out on the rim of Ortygia
      & the mouth of the Cäyster
      & the 7 flumes of the Nile at the delta;
What are all these marvels

21 At Cyzicus there was a statue of Cybele made of hippopotamus
teeth.

before the miracle of Rome?
What riches the earth bears, nature placed here.
   Our warlike rectitude
   is a glory without shame,
for we stand over the world
     with iron & piety; conquest tempered by justice.
Here we have the Anio streaming beside Tibur,
  & the Clitumnus running down out of Umbria;
and the Marcian aqueduct will probably last forever;
   & here is a fine lake below Albanus,
   & Lake Nemi floats under a cloud of leaves;
   & wholesome water flows from that godly spring,
    water trough of Pollux' horse.
Here glide no horned serpents, no scaly bellies here,
   no angry prodigies churn in our pools,
  no Andromedan chains rattle for maternal sin,
nor does Apollo turn his light from our banquets,[22]
   here no son is consumed in a far-off mother's fire,[23]
in Rome no pack of bacchantes
   ever howled under Pentheus' tree,
no Danaän fleet ever set loose from here
   after such dear sacrifice,[24]
nor has Juno the strength
   to bend horns onto a whore's head
   or demean loveliness with bovinity.[25]
Nor do we here record stories
   of sinister trees bent

---

[22] When Atreus killed Thyestes' children and served their flesh to Thyestes at a feast, the sun turned away its light in horror and left the world in darkness.

[23] Meleager's mother burned a piece of wood on which his life depended.

[24] The sacrifice of Iphigenia.

[25] See Io in glossary.

to wrench men asunder,[26]
Or Greek ships welcomed onto cliff rock,[27]
keel timbers curved to their ruin.
Here, Tullus,
   is where you came into the light,
   here is your most lovely home;
In Rome there are honors
      to be won
      worthy of your ancestors,
      worthy citizens awaiting your eloquence;
Here an expectation of grandsons,
      & the well-earned love
      of a future bride.

[26] Sinis was a robber on the isthmus of Corinth who tied his victims to two trees bent toward each other; when the trees rebounded to normal position the victim was torn apart.
[27] See NAUPLIUS in glossary.

23

So it seems
  that my writing tablets
    which taught me so much
have come to ruin
    along with some pretty good verses
      written thereon.
My stylus has worn those tablets down
    with much use,
      & they bore certain verities
even if uncertified
    by wax & signet.
And they could soothe my girlfriends
    even when I wasn't around
      with eloquent verbiage;
They were not precious by gold affixed,
    being made of ordinary boxwood
    & old wax;
Nevertheless, I could always trust them;
    they were always worthy
      of the good things they won.
Sometimes they bore these words,
    returned to me:
"Certainly I am angry,
    seeing that you were most leisurely yesterday
      about coming;
    Perhaps she is more beautiful?
      Or were you strewing lies
        concerning my character?"
Or another time:
    "You will come today,
      & we will lie alone in idleness;

Eros prepares the night's festivities."
These words, & whatever else a quick & verbal girl
might invent in her desires,
when she devises the hour
with alluring guile.
Ah, but now some covetous merchant
inscribes his accounts in them,
puts them in his monstrous files.
Any man bringing them back
will have gold for his trouble;
who would keep firewood
when he could have
a fistful of coins?
Boy, stir yourself & put this notice
on some pillar
& write that your master
inhabits the Esquiline.

24

You worship a faltering flame,
    your beauty is illusion, woman,
   my eyes have made you vain.
Love praised you excessively, Cynthia,
    & now my face burns
      that my verses glorified your loveliness.
I often sang
      your manifold attractions
         so well put together;
Love considered it true beauty,
    not mere appearance.
I often rhapsodized on the radiance of your looks,
    an excellent counterfeit
      of the pale red light
of the morning star;
    but it was the glow of artifice,
         sheen of paint and cosmetic.
My father's friends couldn't turn me away from you,
    & no witch in Thessaly
      could have drowned my desire
   in the whole salt ocean.
This I acknowledge without compulsion forced
      by iron or fire,
        as a man swamped in trouble's running sea.
I was seized by Aphrodite
      & I burned in her crucible;
   She locked my arms, bound them
      in the small of my back.
But as with a garlanded ship
anchored safely in port
    seething riptides & Syrtes' shoals crossed,
      so now I am safe

having found my wits
    with my wounds healing up.
O Right Reason,
    if there is such a goddess,
    I dedicate myself to your shrine
since Father Jupiter stood silent in heaven
        when I lifted my prayers
            for his ears.

Derision & laughter
  at my expense,
      jokes
    on the part
    of whoever would cackle at your banquets;
And I was reasonably faithful,
       your slave for half a decade.
But you will fling down your tears
    & bite your nails
      at loyalty departed
when I leave you;
and I am not moved by tears,
        it was by their artful flow
        I was gotten to this state—
you never wept, except in ambush.
  My eyes will trickle also
      as I swerve onto a new path,
but injury breaks my sorrow—
    you never tolerated any padding for my chains.
Therefore I say good-bye
    to your doors still tearstained at my words,
     the doors I never broke
       with my fist in anger.
May your hidden years oppress you,
    May the coming years line your face,
      years when your passion
will consist only in hating your own white hair.
  Ah, will your mirror applaud
     your withered features
     or will any man?
Can you endure rejection,

scorn coming the other way?
Perhaps, shriveled with time
    you will repent what you have done.
You might consider it possible,
    for it has happened before
        to others.
I sing only a curse now.

BOOK IV

1

This present view, friend, where proud Rome rises
    was grass and high ground prior to Aeneas,
and the Palatine, sacred to Phoebus of ships
      pastured Evander's fugitive herd,
    & our present golden shrines
    come from clay gods.
In the old days no opprobrium lay
      in living in a rude house,
    & the god of the Tarpeian hill
      coughed from an empty cliff,
    & the Tiber was a trough for no cows,
    & where steps ascend to Remus's temple
      a hearth was once boundary
        of the brotherly kingdom.
The senate, gleaming from its hill
      & now full of lordly togas
        once held fur-clad men with rustic hearts.
A crooked horn gathered the antique citizens
      in wordy assembly,
    & a hundred men in a meadow made a quorum.
No sinuous curtains then swung
      over the concave theater,
nor did the stage smell of saffron on feast days.
    No one went whoring
      after foreign gods, and the crowds trembled in suspense
      at their ancestor's rites.
Kindled hay lit the yearly feast of the Pales in those days,

(that rite now revived with the spilling of horse blood)
& impoverished Vesta took pleasure
in wreaths on her asses,
    while lean cattle pulled modest ikons;
Crosspaths were purified
        with the blood of fat pigs
        & peasants offered sheepguts to the tune of reed pipe;
& hide-clad plowmen laid about with rough whips,
    for the rites of Lupercus were in no way restrained.
Those rude soldiers didn't glitter in armor,
    but mixed it up naked,
        with burnt stakes for spears.
The riches of Tatius were a wealth of sheep.
And from all this came the 3 tribes of Rome,
        & the shining team of Romulus.
But our Romans now bear but the name,
    & are embarrassed at having in them
        the blood of the wolf's nursling.
O Troy, the gods exiled from your fireplaces
        were well sent here; the birds were auspicious
        for the landing of your ships;
the fir-wood horse had left us undamaged then,
    at the time when the old man clung to his son's neck,
    and no flame burnt Aeneas' godly shoulders.
Then came the great-souled Decii, & the axes of Brutus,
        & Dione herself bore Caesar's arms,
victorious arms out of the fire of Troy.
    This blessed earth received your gods, Julus,
        & shaking Sibyl, from the tripod,
            ordered Remus to sacrifice on this ground;
& the steady song of Troy's oracle
        to old Priam
has been borne out latterly.
    She warned them, saying:

[202]

"Wheel round your horses, Greeks, your conquest is ill-
       favored;
 Ilium will live, & Zeus will raise arms out of these ashes."
And what great walls
   have come down from the martial wolf,
    best guardian of our affairs.
May I honor these walls with a great song,
  but my voice rings weak;
   yet however thin the stream from my heart
    may it be in Rome's service.
Let Ennius wreathe his verse with a rough crown,
   but extend me your ivy, Bacchus,
    that my books may bring honor to Umbria,
    that Umbria may father Rome's Callimachus.
Assisi's citadel will rise out of the valley
   with greater glory
    as a consequence of my genius.
O Rome, favor me, this surge of oratory is on your behalf.
Citizens, give me a favoring sign; let the bird sing
  a good augury for my undertaking.
& I will sing the fall of Troy, & the raising up of Rome,
  & I will sing tombs in the earth
    & in the far-running sea
& I will sing of sacred days, & the ancient names of places—
 all this must be the goal of my sweating horses.
. . . .
"Misguided poet, where are you going,
  to speak of Fate without foreknowledge?
Your threaded work comes from no well-omened distaff.
  Lamentation will go with your singing, your own
   lamentation.
For Apollo turns away from you;
  you will wring a song from an unwilling lyre
   to your own disadvantage.

[203]

I will bring you the truth, or I am a most ignorant oracle,
    a prophet who cannot read the signs of the brass wheel.
I, Horos, am begotten of Archytas
        of the race of Orops of Babylon.
Conon was ancestor of our house
    & I have not fallen off from my kinsmen,
        the gods witness it,
truth comes foremost in my book.
    Nowadays the gods are made to have a price;
        Zeus is fallen for gold;
and they sell the signs gotten
        from the slanting wheel of the night sky
    & the lucky star of Zeus and the hard light of Mars,
        even the deadly light of Saturn
            will they turn to a profit;
        they explicate the moving stars of Pisces for a price,
            & the windy constellation Leo,
        & Capricorn washed in the waters of sunset.

"I foretold it when Arria bore twin boys
    (given weapons despite God's veto)
        that they would never bring their javelins home
to their ancestral gods,
    and two grave mounds now give credence to that prophecy.
Lupercus fell by his horse with his face bloodied,
        & Gallus was cut down
        before the bloody hook of his eagle standard;
    two funerals from motherly avarice.
My predictions unwelcome, but fell out true.
And when Lucina dragged out Cinara's pains,
        delayed the burden of her womb,
    I said 'let her pray to Juno' & by god she delivered;
        the gift owing to my arcane knowledge.
"Such knowledge is not unrolled to Ammon in his sandy cave,

nor got from entrails spread out for the gods
nor from the flight of birds,
nor from shadows drifting up from magic pools;
Truth is unwound from the ribbon of the sky,
in the path of the stars,
Truth lies in the 5 zones of heaven
exclusively.
In the way of exemplary instances,
recall Calchas to mind,
who loosed ships that might better
have stayed moored to their rocks;
he stained the iron
with the blood of Agamemnon's child
& that blood stained Greek sails;
nor yet did the Danaäns return.
But restrain your grief, O smoking Troy,
look back at Attica's bays.
Nauplius raised up his avenging fire
under the night sky
& the spoil-heavy Greek ships
went down with their booty,
& no more can Ajax rape & carry off Troy's oracle;
Minerva would not let her be torn from her robe.
But enough of old stories.
I turn to your stars now; attend to that dismal tale.
In old Umbria you were born
to an honorable family,
Umbria where the fog from Mevania
strikes the hollow plain with dew,
where Lake Umbria warms with the summer,
& where the towers of Assisi
rise above the hilltops—
ramparts to be glorious with your song?
Do I go wrong in my story, or do I

touch your homeland?
And you had not spent your youth yet
  when you carried your father's cinders,
 & circumstances drove you to thinner Lares.
And whereas once a plenitude of oxen turned your land,
  Caesar's measuring pole [1] removed those tended fields.
But when you took off the gold amulet [2]
  and assumed the toga of freedom
before your mother's gods, at that time Apollo taught you
     some tunes
  & forbade you to rave from the Forum.
To mold & hammer the elegiac song
  is your appointed job—a treacherous undertaking—
but that is your camp.
  And with your example a flock of tunesmiths will come
      following after.
And you will endure hard combat under the arms of
      Aphrodite;
  You will be a strong contender with Eros;
But whatever victories your wars procure you,
    one girl will elude you.
And you will not break her hook, not by courage
    or by fighting the barbed shaft in your soul.
Whether you will close out the light from your eyes at night
    will be her decision,
  and you will weep at her orders.
A thousand spying guardians before her door
   could not help you,
    a small cleft will suffice.
Now whether your ship labors in a heavy sea

[1] "Caesar's measuring pole" refers to land confiscations after the Perusian War.
[2] The gold amulet was worn by sons of noble families.

or you walk unarmed among sword-bearers,
or the earth tremble and draw open
beware above all the 8-footed Crab
of the zodiac." [3]

[3] The Crab of the zodiac is an allusion to Cynthia's greed, since those
born under the Crab were thought greedy.

2

The words of the god Vertumnus:

Multiform, but of one substance,
   I preach my own changes;
      let no man wonder at them.
A Tuscan god, I arose in Tuscan morning,
      but I forsook those fire hearths
         in the wars,
& I am unrepentant over my leaving.
It is this crowd delights me,
     no fane with ivory
       here before the Forum.
Tiberian water flowed here once,
     & oars pulsed in the shallows.
But the river yielded
     to the river's children, & they found a god
       in the river turning,
         called me Vertumnus.
And the new fruit of the cycling year is mine,
      for you know the change in things;
the grapes swell purple for me,
        for me the wheat spike ripens;
      they bring here sweet cherry offerings,
       canicular blackberries, red-gleaming autumn plums;
        here, the payment of fruit grafters,
     wreathed fruit in vow payment,
     when the pear trunk surrenders apples.
I pray Rumor's silence.
Other mutations go with my name; hear it & believe.
  I know all forms
       & will ornament any shape you will have me take.
In a Coan cape, a pretty girl;

in a toga, none would gainsay my virility.
Give me a sickle & headband twisted from grass,
      & you will call me a mower, swear it by oath.
I once bore arms & in arms won honor
    but with head-balanced basket I became again a reaper.
I am all sobriety in the courtroom,
    but with the wreath set for drinking
        you will giggle at my wine-drunk stumble.
Crown me with a miter & I will counterfeit Bacchus;
I am Apollo with the plectrum,
    a hunter with the snare;
with the reed I am the fowler's god;
I am a charioteer, a mounted acrobat.
With a cane pole I pull forth fish
    & I will go into the world
      with a long tunic, an elegant huckster.
I know how to lean on the herdsman's bent stick,
    & carry roses & asafetida in the dust.
And gardens are my great glory,
    thus the gifts before me, cucumbers, gourds, cabbages,
        these my insignia.
Nor does any flower stand open
        that will not grow languid handsomely
brought from the field to my wreath.
My name came from manifold forms;
    the shapes of the Latin tongue
        became my shapes.
And Rome has rewarded my homeland,
      turned a pathway into Tuscany Street;
This gift after Lucumo bruised the Sabines.
    I saw ranks turned & spears thrown down,
      & the rear side of their armor.

I have been

a whittled maple post, in ancient times,
    a poor god in a pleasing town,
but may earth spare Mamurius,
      graver of bronze, who poured another shape
for Vertumnus, one work with many honors.
But may the god who begot the rest
    keep this toga'd crowd
  before my feet
      throughout all time.

3

Arethusa sends this message
  to her husband Lycotas—
   if you may be called mine,
  being so much absent—
If some words are unclear,
  my tears render them so;
  should the letters seem ill-formed
   and uncertain,
  it is my right hand
   trembling in weakness.
Bactra beneath the rising sun
  beholds once more your presence,
and you are familiar to the Neuric army
   & their mailed horses,
  and to the icebound Getae, & Britain of the painted cars,
  and to the burning waves
  of multicolored India under the morning star.
Is this the marital faith
  pledged with the night's kisses
   when I was an awkward girl
& gave you my embrace, arms conquered by your wishes?
On my wedding night the torchlight flared ill-omened;
  a black flame from some torn-down funeral fire;
I was sprinkled from a pool of hell,
  nor was riband set right in my hair;
  no god floated with my veil.
I have hung offerings from all the gates,
  I weave now your fourth war cloak,
and O I hope oblivion was that man's fate
  who first raised a palisade
  hewn from harmless trees,
& contrived the shrill-boned war fife.

Better he to sit at one end of a rope
    than Ocnus obliquely feeding
       the small ass always.
Tell me, my husband,
    does the cuirass chafe your shoulders,
       & the weight of the javelin
    blister your peaceable hands?
I would hope for these injuries
      & not the work of some girl's teeth;
      such neck wounds would hurt me also,
        leave me in tears.
They say your face gets thin;
      I hope your pallor
    is from wishing for me.
When the ashen night
      spreads over me at sundown,
I kiss left-behind weapons,
    and the bedcovers
      will not stay put on the bed,
& the birds before dawn are late to sing.
In the winter night I labor at the loom,
    purple wool for the life of the garrison,
    Tyrian cloth for the life of the sword;
I teach myself where the Araxes flows,
        that river you must conquer,
and inquire as to the mileage of Parthian horses
       between water holes;
& I study the world as laid out on the maps,
      the location of high Dahan,
        which land hardens with frost,
        which crumbles with heat;
I know which wind will drive your sails toward Italy.
And here

one sister comforts me
in my distraction,
and a pale nurse swears falsely
that it is winter keeps you.
How I envy Hippolyte! Bare-breasted she wore the sword
& curled her soft hair
beneath cruel battle crown;
I wish only that Rome
let women march with the legions,
and I would go to war with you
as faithfully as your pack;
no ridge in Scythia would stop me,
even when God steels deep water
in ice and cutting cold.
Love is a strong god always,
strongest in a true husband's wife;
It is Aphrodite breathes on this flame,
that it might live.
What good to me is shining purple,
& bright crystal in hand?
All things fall silent now,
& are without hearing,
and only with the rare kalends
does the regular girl uncloset the Lares.
The small dog's whine pleases me,
my only bedmate now;
I cover the shrines with flowers
& enshroud the crossroads
with sacred branches,
and Sabine herbs crackle
in the ancient altar fire.
And if the owl note sounds
from a nearby roof beam

or the low-burning lamp needs a wine offering,
    then it is time that this year's lambs
        go the the altar;
    time then that junior priests gird themselves,
        & warm themselves for new lucre.
Be not too proud, I pray,
    with Bactra beneath you,
        yours the fine linen reft
from their perfumed captains
    after the lead shot from the unwound sling
        is strewn on the battlefield,
& after the cunning bow shots
    have rung from the turning horses.
But in any case, when you have tamed
    Parthia's nurslings
may the headless spear [4] reward your chariot,
    and may you keep our bed covenant unbroken;
    May these circumstances attend your return.
I will at that time
    carry your war gear
        & offerings
        to the Capene gate
& inscribe beneath them:

FOR HIS SAFE RETURN

FROM A FAITHFUL WIFE

[4] The headless spear was a kind of medal for meritorious service.

[214]

4

These words lifted up
    over the stained tomb,
      the sacred trees of Tarpeia,
        the taken gates of ancient Jupiter.
Tatius ringed this mountain, planted a palisade
      of maple posts
      & raised his own tents behind dirt ramparts.
What was Rome then, when Cures' hornblower
    broke his long notes
        on godly cliffs hard by;
          when Sabines racked their spears in the Forum
            where Rome now hands down law to empire?
Hills were Rome's towers
    and the armored horse drank
      at a thin spring
        where the Senate sits now.
And in that place
    a fruitful grove
      secret in an ivied cleft
        where the trees sounded against native springs,
branch & reed pipe, Sylvanian home,
      the sheep went to the music
        to a shadowed well,
& Tarpeia, clay jar on her head,
    came down
      to bring water for Vesta;
& there she caught sight of that king, Tatius,
        on maneuver in a sandy plain,
      damasked iron raised over gold crests.
And struck by the regal countenance
    & kingly armor

she let the jar fall forgotten
from strained hands.
Ah, Vesta, is one doom sufficient
for a priestess oblate to another flame?
And Tarpeia swore, in more than one night,
that the clear moon rose
with evil meaning,
& again, & again, she went down to the stream
to tinge her hair therein;
and came often before alluring nymphs,
blades of silver lilies in her hands;
this that her king receive no wound from Romulus.
Mornings she ascended the great hill
overcast with early smoke,
& came home evenings arms scarred by the thorn.
And on her citadel she lamented wounds
no god might cure:
"O God, if only I sat before
the fires of his garrison,
before the main tent,
Sabine swords gleaming in my eyes.
If only I lay captive,
& as a prisoner saw his face.
I bid you good-bye, high hills, & also Rome
crowning those hills,
good-bye to Vesta,
who will redden at my disgrace.
That stallion he rides, whose mane he smooths,
will lay my desires to rest among his tents.
Who will stand in amazement
that Scylla clipped her father's hair;
what wonder that a sister betrayed
the Minotaur's hideous horns,
revealing the twisted way with loom thread unstrung?

I will bring shame to the beauties of Italy
    but I was not cut out
    to tend this virgin flame.
  Let that man who is astonished forgive me;
    my tears run down the altar.
The word passes
  that tomorrow they sanctify the city.
  Take, then, the dew-struck back
    of the brambled ridge, a slick trail,
    & treacherous, hiding quiet watery pitfalls.
O if I knew the chants of magic's goddess
  my words would serve your splendor
    with deeds.
You deserve
  the lordly toga, not that man of no mother
    who sucked the wolf-bitch teat.
Shall I then not be your queen, & bear children
  in your inner court?
  I bring a suitable dowry,
    I bring you Rome betrayed.
If I shall not be your wife, rape me then
  & requite in turn your own ruined women.
But I can break the cutting edge
  of armies set afoot.
I can bring brides to the covenant
  with my marriage robe;
Hymenaeus, lift up your measures;
  trumpeter, put away that wild music.
Lend belief to it, believe it, when I ornament your bed
  I will gentle your sword.
Now the fourth horn sings coming light,
  & the stars glide down seaward,
    I will search for sleep,
      search for you in dreams,

may your visage come lovely to my eyes."
Thus she spoke, relinquished to an uncertain dream,
   without foreknowledge of what furies lay in wait.
Vesta, holy guard of the Trojan coals,
     fanned the fire in her bones,
        augmented sin;
   & Tarpeia rose and rushed down
like an Amazon by roaring Thermodon
   robe torn & breast laid bare.
And now in the city,
     ancient festival, ancestral Parilia,
     celebration of the early walls—
       a yearly banquet, feast of herdsmen,
    engorgements & games, drunken throngs dancing
         dirty-footed among piles of burning straw.
And the decree of Romulus came then:
abandon the guard posts,
    put down the trumpet.
Thus she reckoned the time come,
   & made fast the pact,
     herself part of the bargain.
Now her king, the slick hill ascended, the guard gone to the
                         feast,
    fell on the watchdogs, iron to the windpipe.
And all the city slept but Jupiter, the god wakeful over
                    retribution;
    the fatherland handed over thus,
     the trust of the gate broken;
    for she sought the bridal veil.
And the king (who at that point
    abjured treason)
   invited her to a royal couch
   & ordered her broken under shields.

BOOK IV

This for the dowry,
 and from her the hill is named,
 her night watch thus rewarded with injustice.[5]

[5] I have not rendered well in English the ambiguity in the final line
of this occasionally touching poem.

[219]

5[6]

May brambles rise from the earth
    to cover your slattern tomb;
   may your ghost float dry,
    thirst being your hell.
      May a triple-throated hungry howl out of Erebus
        haunt your rotten bones.
This witch, she could have lured Hippolytus to bed,
      but to no harmonious bed,
    she was always an ill-omened bird for harmony.
She could have lured Penelope to wed
    with lewd Antinoüs,
      whispers of Ulysses alive notwithstanding.
At her will, the lodestone would unclamp iron,
    a bird abandon nestlings;
      and if she bring magic herbs to her ditch,
        then firm things dissolve into water.
She would enchant the moon
    with her brazen magical song;
   she would roam by night in a wolf's shape
      that husbands might be undone, deceit
      blinding their watch
        stretched out anxious through the night.
And with crow's eyes
    & the counsel of screech owls
   she sought my blood,
    and gathered potions for my seed
      from the effluence of pregnant mares.
And she kept at her work, underminer,
    like a mole in hard ground,
    & she would advise Cynthia thus:

[6] Ovid borrowed a good deal from this poem.

"If the dawn-gold shore of Dorozantum delights you,
   or the proud purple dye of Tyrian conch;
   if kingly Coan silk pleases you,
     and cut figurines languid with gold ornament,
     & gifts from palmy Thebes, & fired ceramic chalices
       out of Parthia,
then sidestep good faith; & for god's sake
     live in no odor of sanctity,
    make no ruinous covenant wth chastity.
And by no means rely on truth.
   Pretend you have hooked another man,
    use any device.
Love burns stronger if you scatter out his nights.
If he takes you by the hair in anger,
   make use of the anger,
       press him to buy back love's promise
        when he wants it,
     and then feign obliged abstinence
      for the overdue rites of Isis.
Have your servant inform you then
    of the upcoming Feast of Courtesans
      requiring celebration,
    & let another harp on your impending birthday;
     He will then pray your attention.
Sit and pretend to write someone;
   if he trembles,
     you know you have him.
Never hide the bites on your neck,
   & he will speculate as to what struggling produced them.
But avoid Medea's transgression—disdained
    for asking first.
Instead imitate worldly Menander's high-priced whore.
Change your custom with the man.

If he prides his singing,
      lift your voice to his sotted tune.
Have the doorman stand alert
      for those who bring gifts,
but have him sleep through empty-handed knocks,
      have him sleep with the bolt drawn.
Take on soldiers when they come,
      even if as rough in love as war,
take sailors when they grip coppers
      in calloused hands;
Hell, take chalk-footed barbarians [7]
      who have danced in the slave market.
Examine carefully the gold,
not the hand the gold arrives in.
      And if you attend verses, what will you gain but words?
      'Why go forth in the streets
      with elegant coiffure, my love,
      moving in subtle curves of Coan vestment?'[8]
Hear no man who gives you Coan verses
      instead of Coan silk, & learn to grow deaf
      to the ungilded lyre.
Use your time while the blood pumps strong
and your beauty is unmarred by wrinkles,
      before that future morning
when your face will please no man.
I have beheld the blight, the burning of rose gardens
      under the morning wind out of Africa."
And while Acanthis thus twisted my Cynthia's soul,
      you could have counted my bones
      under my taut skin.

---

[7] It was customary to whiten the feet of slaves put up for sale.
[8] This quotation is possibly an interpolation of the first three lines of I.2.

But receive my gift in your fire, Queen Aphrodite,
I saw her cough harden in her wrinkled throat,
  bloody spittle in hollow teeth;
I saw her evil soul expire,
  a chill in the broken fireplace of her brothel.
Her funeral riches were two stolen headbands,
 a pale miter ruined by neglect,
  & that overwakeful dog of painful memory,
  always alert
   when my hands would unloose the grating.
Let this jade's grave marker be
  a cracked amphora;
 may the fig tree grow out of her ashes;
 and all you who love, whoever you are,
  fall on that sepulcher
   with stones and maledictions.

6

Let there be silence, that the sacrifice fall well;
    the heifer is struck down now
    before the fire of my altar,
        with properly inspired consecration.
Let the Roman wreath contend
    with the ivy berries of Philetas,
  let the jar splash me
        with Cyrenian water,[9] give me
        mild myrrh & alluring olibanum,
& wind the wool disk [10] 3 times round the fire;
    pour the ablution down,
        let the ivory flute
          ring a tuneful song
    here by the new altar;
Deception, depart; let evil float in another air.
    Smooth the singer's new path with laurel.
Muse, we will bring anew
    the story of Palatine Apollo's shrine; Calliope,
    the work deserves your favor.
I sing these songs in Caesar's name,
    & while Caesar is sung, I pray even Zeus be silent.
The scene: The Athamanian coast, the shore of Apollo,
    a sheltering bay out of Ionian sea rumble;
    Actium's sea, a relief to sailors,
    a memorial to Julian craft.
Here the fleets of the world assembled,
    great bulks of pine, stock-still on the water.
The bird of providence failed one side,
    one fleet to be ruined by Trojan Augustus,

[9] A reference to Callimachus
[10] A festoon of wool often seen carved on Roman altars.

for the shame of a Roman lance in the hands of a woman.
And under conquering insignia
    sails tightened
       in Jovian blessing,
& Nereus bent the twin ranks in a sharp crescent,
    & the painted water shimmered
       in the radiation of arms.
And Phoebus came out of Delos—now rooted in the sea
    under his shield, though once floating
       with the rage of the south wind—
stood above the august poop deck
    with slanting torch fire,
       a curved triple flame.
No loose hair then, no strung tortoise shell;
but he looked as he did when he shot death
    through Agamemnon's camp,
    & as when he broke the turning coils of the Python,
       terror of pacific Muses.
"O Augustus," said he, "descended from Alba Longa,
    Preserver of the world, renowned above Hector,
    the land is yours, conquer now in sea wave.
My bow bends in your service,
    the bolts at my shoulder favor you.
  Unshackle the country from fear,
    the country puts prayers on your keel.
If you should not defend Rome,
    then the birds Romulus saw from the Palatine
    portended evil for his walls.
The enemy rows too close.
Must Latin billows uphold a queen
  while you are prince? Have no fear, though their fleet
    move on winged oars,
  those ships will move only to the sea floor.
Despite prows with centaurs & rock-wielding monsters,

you will prove them hollow timbers & painted terrors.
The strength of a soldier is broken or lifted
   by the strength of his cause,
     with no justice in his cause, a soldier's sword shakes in
      his hand.
Now it is time; for I create the time,
   commit your fleet, & I will lead it with the laurel bough."
And they felt the weight of his bow,
     and the bite of Caesar's lance,
& Rome came back victorious
   with Apollo's help; and that woman
     was brought to ruin; the Ionian floated broken scepters.
Augustus, from godly Caesar's blood, under Caesar's comet,
     was sung by Triton & Nereid,
      & they applauded the banners of liberty.
And the Queen pulled wickedly
   for the river Nile,
   the one goal she achieved,
     & she chose her own time to die.
Which is for the best; how would it look
   to lead a woman through the same streets
     Jugurtha came through?
Thus Actian Phoebus got his monument—
   pay for his boat-breaking projectiles.
I have sung sufficiently of war;
  Apollo would now hear my cithern;
   he lays down his sword for the quiet dance.
Let the glittering banquet pass into the grove,
   & alluring roses circle my neck.
Pour the Falernian, put perfume in my hair;
   & may the Muse inflame poets now heated only with
     drink—
Phoebus & Bacchus go well together.
Let's have some

poet
    retell the breaking of the Sycambri,
or sing of the black kingdom beyond the Nile,
    or the truce with the Parthians, thus:
"Bring home the Roman standards; they will lose their own
      soon enough.
    or if Caesar spares the East, it will be as a trophy
      for his grandsons.
Rejoice, Crassus, if the light has not yet left you
    in the black sands
      that we can now pass over the Euphrates
      to your graveyard."
Thus with libation the night passes,
    with Propertius as cheerleader,
until the morning sunray strikes my wineglass.

7[11]

Spirits float in the night
    liberated by death,
        that illusion of finality.
The shadowing ghost rises lurid
    from the smoking fire;
Cynthia, just buried in the murmur
    of her last road,
        came in the dark,
    a wraith at my bed, when sleep hovered
    in the wake of love's funeral,
        and I mourned in my cold-couched realm.
Her proud hair was as it once was
    and her eyes
    but her tunic was burnt
        & her beryl ring fire-blackened,
her lovely lips parched
    by the waters of Lethe.
Spirit and whispers
    were carried in her breath,
    fragile hands clicked their bones.
"Dishonest man,
    though you could be worse,
        has a hard sleep gripped you so soon?
Do you forget our intrigues
    in the watching Roman night,
do you forget my window
    polished by our midnight meetings,
        when I came down a rope
hand over hand, landing in your arms?
Oftentimes the two of us & love mingled at the crossroads,
    heartbeat to heartbeat,
    the road hot beneath our cloaks.

[11] This poem has been translated by Robert Lowell.

The southerly squalls sweep deaf to our silent love pact,
    those lies whipped off with the wind.
No man grieved as the light left my eyes,
  and had you prayed
    I might have seen one day more.
No night watchman rattled his cloven cane
    at my departure,
  and my head rested on a broken tile.
    Who saw you at the last,
      bowed at my burial,
    your toga black
      with hot tears?
If being seen in the street with my bier offended you,
    you might have had it carried to the door
    more slowly.
Why didn't you pray for a wind
    to fan the fire, ungracious man?
Why didn't the flame smoke with incense?
  And what a great burden
    the price of a few hyacinths would have been,
    a few flowers for the fire,
  and an offering from a broken flask.

"And let Lygdamus burn, let the iron grow incandescent
    for my slave, whose crime I sensed
as I paled at his wine;
    & let Nomas remove
    her hidden concoctions;
the cup burning with venom
    will brand her hands.
That doxy, the object of the public's gaze
    because of her price, which was cheap,
    now dusts the ground
with a golden gown. She repays the honest words
    of a servant who has praised my beauty

with heavier work;
& Petale is chained for carrying
    a flower crown to my headstone;
& Lalage is hung up by her braided hair & whipped
    for daring to say my name.
And you let her melt my golden image
    so she might have a dowry from my flames.
Yet I will not press these complaints,
    though you deserve to hear them,
for I reigned a long while
    in the kingdom of your books.
Let the 3-headed dog howl more softly,
    for I swear by the Fates, whose song cannot be undone,
        that I was faithful,
and if I lie
    may a snake coil hissing over my bones.
Hell allots two places
        beside its black river
    and all who come
must be rowed to one or the other,
    through those clamoring waters.
One barge is stained by Clytemnestra's crime,
    bears the monstrous carved horns
        of Pasïphaë.
But behold the flowered yawl
    sailing others to Elysium
        where rich winds stir the roses gently,
where the lutes strum
    & Cybele's bronze cymbals ring,
        where mitered dancers move to the lyre.
Andromeda and Hypermnestra,
    pure and blameless wives,
        recount their adventures there;

Andromeda speaking of arms bruised by chains,
  hands wrongly locked to the cold rock;
And Hypermnestra of the bold crimes of her sisters
  & how she quailed at such evil.
Thus with the tears of death
  we heal life's loves.
But I keep your faithless ways secret still.
    But now see to these things,
      if your heart has stirred,
if the philters of your present whore
  have not laid hold of you:
Let my nurse Parthenie have
  whatever she might want
    in her trembling age;
She was neither harsh nor avaricious.
  Forbid my dear Latris
    to hold up the mirror to another mistress.
And burn the songs you wrote for me;
  cease to use my fame.
Dislodge the ivy from my tomb
  which twists its leaves and berries
    around my yielding bones.
And where the fruitful Anio
  curls through the orchards
    where ivory whitens with age,[12]
by order of Hercules,
    there, in Tibur, inscribe a song worthy of me
      in stone, but briefly,
        that it may be read
      from the running chariot
      by the traveler from the city:

[12] Ivory was thought to grow whiter with age in the air of Tibur.

HERE LIES GOLDEN CYNTHIA
IN HER TIBURTINE FIELDS
SHE ADDS TO THE ANIO'S GLORY

And do not fear these holy dreams;
          they come with truth.
Night frees us and we walk shadowy abroad,
          Cerberus himself howls straying in the night.
But the dawn requires our return
                    to the marshes of hell
                    & we come and are counted by the ferryman.
Now may some other woman have you
for soon
          you will be mine again,
                    bone against polished bone."
Her reproaches ended then
          and her smoky image
          vanished as I embraced it.

8

Hear me, and learn
    what pulse of alarm
        struck through the night of the liquid Esquiline,[13]
propelling a fearful throng through the New Field gardens
    when a foul tumult agitated the darkness,[14]
        tumult in which I meant to be no contender,
      & in which my good name received certain injuries.
Lanuvium is from old times guarded by her tutelary snake,
    an ageless reptile; a pause there is worth your while,
    a pause for this distinguished attraction.
Sacred steps plunge down a black cleft there,
    down which his yearly sacrifice descends,
      when reptilian hunger requires propitiation
(Young woman, beware of such places)
      when his annual hisses curl from the hollow earth.
A pale virgin descends to lurid rites,
    hands held out rashly with provender
        for his honorable maw,
    canister clattering in fearful hands.
If she be chaste, she returns to her parents' arms
       & the farmers sing that it will be a prosperous year,
        a fertile year.
My Cynthia took herself there, wth gleaming horses,
      pleading Juno's worship, intending Aphrodite's,
her chariot hurtling over the rocks,
    wheels reckless on the Appian Way,
Cynthia suspended at the pole's head, a spectacular sight,
      whipping her way through the bad spots in the road
      with somewhat more daring than the average beardless

13 The slopes of Esquiline Hill were marshy and full of springs.
14 This line and the two that follow translate lines 19 and 20 of the
Latin.

prodigal
in his carriage hung with Chinese silk
& his necklaced poodle.[15]
Thus another of her absences from our bed,
& I undertook a little diversion,
& pitched camp elsewhere.
Two girls, Phyllis, who lives near the Aventine Diana;
who lacks charm sober, although things improve when she
drinks;
& Teia, who resides near the Tarpeian wood,
a glowing beauty, & when she is fired by wine,
half a dozen lovers are scarcely sufficient.
I invited these two, set up a small orgy
to soothe the long night & renew the dormant rites
of Aphrodite
with secret lubricity.
One couch in a hidden garden served for 3 of us,
me between the two,
and Lygdamus manned the wine ladle,
& our summertime equipage of chalices served for the
wine,
a Greek wine, odor of Methymna.
Flutist from the Nile, a treble flute was played that night,
& Phyllis played the castanets, elegantly artless,
pleased to receive roses of acclamation.
Magnus the dwarf hopped and waved his hardened hands
to the fluted descant, song of the hollow boxwood.
The lantern was full; the flame wavered [16] in the night,
the table had collapsed with its burden,
& as the dice clattered I prayed for the Venus throw,
but always the damned dog leapt into the light;
And they sang to a deaf man, & bared their bodies

[15] A short Propertian digression following this line has been omitted.
[16] A wavering flame was an omen of impending arrival.

[234]

for a blind man,
for I was alone at the gates of Lanuvium.
Suddenly a hinge creak at the doorposts,
    loud and resonant, a light footfall at the Lares,
        & then Cynthia threw down the folding doors,
hair disheveled, in a fiery rage.
She smashed the cup from my fingers; my wine-stricken lips
                                                went white,
    her eyes glittered, female rage possessed her;
A city would burn less wildly than she did,
as she sank savage claws in Phyllis's face,
    & Teia's frightful wail floated into the watery environs;
        and the neighbors, aroused,
    raised torches and milled in the street,
& the paths of the night echoed with madness.
My two girls fled, hair torn & tunics loose,
        into the first tavern on the dark road.
Now Cynthia came back, victress, & took a menacing pleasure
        in the spoils she had captured, wounded my mouth
    with her nails & bloodied my neck with her teeth,
& undertook to darken my wandering eyes with her fists;
    & when her arms got tired with that she spied Lygdamus
        cowering by the sinister couch, & she dragged him into
            the light
        as he prayed that I protect him. How can *I* protect you,
Lygdamus, when she has me by the balls?
    With much supplication, she became more reasonable,
        though she would scarcely let me touch her feet.
"If you really want me to forgive this turpitude,
    then you will no longer go strolling
        in the shade of Pompey's colonnade, dressed in
    your best finery; you will abstain from attending
the games in the Forum; you won't loiter about eyeing the
                                            curtainless

palanquins jog past; you will abstain also
from craning your neck at those attractions
 in the high tiers of the theater, and finally,
let Lygdamus, that great troublemaker, be sold;
let his ankle chains clank as he walks."
To all this I acceded, and she smiled proud in her sovereignty,
 and she perfumed the contamination of those others,
  & washed the threshold with clear water,
  had me change my mantle, and with a fire of sulfur
  touched my head 3 times;
and then with the sheets changed
 we ascended into the covers,
 & we rolled over the whole bed,
 & thus resolved our quarrel.

9[17]

In those days, Hercules came on his cattle drive
        out of Erythea,
    came with his stolen cows to the wild hill
        of the Palatine
      hill teeming with herds, and there, being tired
          he camped to graze his cattle & recover strength,
there where the Velabrum widened its waters
        forming a pool,
      boats floating over future urbanity.
But there were no welcome guests, and no cows were safe
    with the monster Cacus abroad, polluting & thieving—
    Cacus being a native of the place,
      a robber from a fearful hole, a giant with three rumbling
          mouths.
    Now Cacus, so the tracks should not betray him,
        & his plundering not be manifest,
      took the cows by their tails, pulled them
        into his cave backward.
    But their bellows gave him away,
        & the god found the robber's cave
    & in anger pulled down the brutal doors.
    And he laid Cacus out with 3 swings of his cudgel,
        one stroke per head.
And Hercules then took leave of his twice-plundered cattle,
    calling them the last work of his club:
    "Let your moos hallow the ox's field,
      & your pasture be the grandeur of the Forum."
But now thirst was afflicting his dry tongue,
      & swarming earth provided no water.
But laughter far off struck his ear, from women behind walls,

[17] This poem and IV.10 are perfunctory and bad, both in Latin and in English, but they may have had a "stuffed-owl" humor for the Romans.

from a coppice circling in a ring of shadows;
 the secret place of the Goddess of Women,
 where the rites were never laid bare without penalty.
The doors were out of the way, & purple ribbons veiled
  them,
 & the crumbling hut shone with perfumed fire,
 & a long-leafed poplar embellished the temple
 & hid birdsong in its shadows.
And he came down to the gate
  dust matting a dry beard, and cast these words
  less exalted than his godly character:
"I pray you, those of you who play
 in the sacred hollow of the grove,
throw open your temple to a tired man looking for a
  drink.
 The waters sound around me as I walk.
 A cupped handful from the stream would do.
Has word not reached you
 of the man who lifted the world on his back?
I am that man, whom the earth calls Hercules.
Who hasn't heard of the great work
 of my stick & of the true aim
 of my beast-killing spear,
and how one man lit black hell?
Receive me; I am tired; this earth is scarcely open to me.
 Even if you serve the altar of bitter Juno,
  she never denied me water.
 If you fear the lion skin
And my hair burnt in African sun,
 remember I once worked as a woman
 with wool & distaff, and a soft breastband
  on my hairy chest,
 and I was a pretty apt girl."
Purple ribbon in her white hair, the priestess replied, in her

kindness:
"Let your eyes not light within
        this venerable grove, depart from it,
    retire & go now, forsake these lintels
        for your own sake.
The altar that claims this secret shrine
        may be seen by no man, & is avenged by fearful
            law.
The seer Tiresias beheld great Pallas naked
        as she bathed, the Gorgon shield laid down;
            & he paid a great price.
    May the gods show you another fountain. This ravine
        bears the secret stream
            of women only."
Thus the old hag.
    But the locked gates buckled under Hercules' thirsty rage,
        and his shoulders broke the doorposts down;
            and he sucked up the stream, to put out the fire.
And then with his lips wiped dry
        he founded a new altar:
"This corner of the world
        now receives me
            in the path of my fate.
    Though I am fatigued, this land is hardly receptive.
I will consecrate this great altar to the
            rescue of my cattle,
        & the altar will be great by my hands.
    But it will never be open to women,
        that Hercules' thirst be remembered
            in coming ages."
And because Hercules had cleansed the world,
        he was established in this altar
            by Tatian Cures.
Hail, father Herakles, whom wild Juno favors now;
        favor my book.

[239]

10

I will undertake now,
    to lay bare the beginnings
      of Feretrian [18] Jupiter;
  the triple loot of weapons seized
      from three generals.
I climb the great road, but glory gives me the strength—
  no crown from an easy ridge can please me.
Romulus first knew the value of spoils;
    Romulus, you first brought plunder home,
    that time you broke Acron's army
      which would have seized our gates;
your lance point nailed him
      to his own horse.
Acron, seed of Hercules, commander of Caenina's citadel,
    once carried fear to the borders of Rome;
  he wanted spoils from the shoulders of Romulus,
  but he was himself relieved of his armor,
      stained with his own blood.
They met before the hollow towers,
    spears balanced, & Romulus went first
      with spear & vow,
  "Zeus, today this sacrifice on your altar,"
  & Acron fell the spoil of Jupiter.
Father of Rome and of manly virtue,
    Romulus was used to conquest,
      coming from thin Lares & cold tents;
        as apt at the plow
        as at the bridle;
his helmet was a wolf hide with a bushy crest;
his painted buckler shone

[18] This poem hinges on a pun on *Feretrius, fero,* and *ferire.* Like H. E. Butler, I cannot translate it.

[240]

with no overlay of bronze; his belt was uncured leather.
The sound of Roman war had not yet
        gone over the Tiber,
    the farthest conquest being Nomentum & 3 acres in Cora.
    Then came Cossus, who cut down Tolumnius of Veii,
        in the days when conquering Veii,
            was no small thing.
Ah, ancient Veii, you were then a kingdom
    with a gold throne in your market.
Now lazy shepherds bray on crooked horns
        among your walls, & farmers harvest among your
            bones.
Tolumnius stood above the gates,
        trusting in his fortress,
    while the ram struck the walls, with brassy horn,
        & the mantlet covered the siege line.
And Cossus shouted
    "Better for brave men to meet in open field"
        & soon
            two ranks stood poised on the plain.
And the gods came to the aid of the Latin side;
    Tolumnius' throat cut, his blood spattering Roman horses.
And after that,
        Claudius beat the enemy
    back over the Rhone they had overshot,
    & brought home the rude shield of Virdomarus,
            their general,
        who boasted his Rhenish origin.
Virdomarus drove a straight chariot
& wielded a Gaulish javelin;
    & he fell in his striped pants
        in mid march,
        the bent torque cut from his neck.

Now the shrine
    bears
       triple plunder, this, & the generals
      borne down
    by the sword, & the arms
      borne home,
bear the story of the temple's name.

11

Leave my tombstone dry, Paullus,
   no tears, no prayers,
    may bring down the black gate,
once we are laid under dust
    in hell's jurisdiction;
     the road is barred after by fired steel.
The Lord of Shadows in his black palace
     may hear your entreaties,
    even so, your tears will evaporate
    in the silences of his coasts.
Beseechments may move Olympia,
   but let the boatman get his copper coins
    and he will bolt and lock
     the unearthly gate
    on his cargo of shades for once and all.
Thus sang the dark tubas with the blaze
    of the somber funeral torch brought down
    as the flame flickered against the couch
     & underneath my head.
What good then was my wedding day,
   & my children with my glory in their faces;
   what worth had my proud ancestral chariots?
They did not keep me
   from the bitter Parcae,
    & I drift as dust through the fingers now.
I do not come to the nights of hell
    and wade in shallow swamps
     with guilt in my heart.
I died young,
and may Lord Death have mercy
   on this phantom of Cornelia.
If Aeacus sits magistrate by the urn of judgment

may he adjudge no punishment
    when my number comes up.
Judges, draw close, let the austere Eumenides align themselves
    by the Minoan throne, and the court be silent.
Stay your boulder, Sisyphus,
    let Ixion be unslung from his rumbling wheel,
Tantalus, assuage your dry throat,
    rattle not your chain, Cerberus,
        leave these specters in peace.
I speak now in my own behalf
    & if I lie let me bear all the urns of the Danaïdes.
Does anciently won glory and ancestral honor count, my
        lords?
  My devices speak of Scipio Africanus,
    and my mother also
      was of good family,
    & my husband's house is thus well founded.
When the bridal torches lit
    my maidenly disrobing, and a new ribbon graced my
        hair, Paullus,
we were long ago united in that bedchamber
    I now am sundered from.
In cut stone read
        TO ONE ONLY WAS SHE A BRIDE
May the holy ashes of my great ancestors
    whose standards ruled in Africa,[19]
be my witnesses.

. . . .

Perses, Achilles in your heart and lineage,
    with Hercules your forebear also,
      who splintered the door of this smoky hall,
Bear witness that I loosened no covenant,

[19] A reference to Scipio Africanus.

no ordinance of my husband, Censor Paullus.
   Nor was our fire darkened by any shame.
Cornelia damned no won splendor of that house,
   her virtue shone out even in such splendor.
I lived
      without accusation, unchanged by the passing years,
      exemplary between the one torch and the other.
Nature ruled law into my marrow;
   I fear no judge,
   let any who will cast a ballot;
   any woman may consider herself undemeaned in my
                                 company,
even you, Claudia, great priestess of the rondel crown;
      and you, Aemilia, votary of Vesta, rekindling
         from dead coals the flame
      with a bright flaxon wand.
Nor have I wounded your sweet head, mother Scribonia;
   what would you wish changed in me, but my present fate?
My mother's tears, and the city's lamentations,
      are my threnody;
My bones are interred with a groan from Caesar,
   & the god whispered that I was a becoming sister
         to his Julia, and went with liquid eye at my death.
I have earned my vestments of honor,[20]
I was not severed from a barren house.
Paullus and Lepidus, you soothe me, you bring solace
   even into hell. The light left my eyes in your bosom.
And I lived to see my brother [21]
   twice seated on the curule throne,
      & it was during the feast of his consulate

[20] I.e., she was awarded the stola of honor for having had more than two children.
[21] P. Cornelius Scipio.

that his sister was taken from celebration.
Daughter, semblance of your father, born to his honors,
    have only one man, after my example.
And sustain our lineage, my children,
    & I will go willing when the boat of hell floats loose,
      having been a mother to such children.
This is my reward and my triumph,
    that the living should exalt my glory,
        lift voice in my praise
           as the pyre's smoke rises.
Now Paullus, I give you these children,
      tokens of our union,
      and this care burns in my bones.
You must discharge my duty to them,
    I bequeath you a crowd of dependents
      & you must bear that burden
    and kiss them for me;
    the house and its work I bequeath to you also.
If grief afflicts you, hide it; and when they come to you
    deceive them, kiss them with a tearless eye.
Often, Paullus, you will lie awake
      thinking of me;
there will be enough nights
    when my beauty will light your dreams;
    and when you speak to me in solitude,
      speak as if I should reply.
Children, if the marriage couch by the door should change
    and a cautious stepmother linger in my stead
uphold and praise your father's choice
    and your propriety will capture her heart.
Do not praise me too much, or she will turn in anger.
    Or if he endures mindful of my spirit
    and esteems my memory always,

take notice of age growing upon him
and leave no way that care might afflict him
in his solitude.
May the time death took from me
be added to your years,
May my children be a delight to Paullus when he is old.
I am thankful, for never did I wear black
for any child of mine,
& they all came to my funeral.
I have spoken my case, witnesses,
Earth will return its reward for my life.
Heaven is accessible to virtue,
& may my bones be carried
among my honored ancestors.

GLOSSARY

ACANTHIS. Procuress and friend of Cynthia.

ACHAEA. Greece.

ACHERON. River in hell, or hell itself.

ACHILLES. Foremost Greek hero of Trojan War.

ACRON. King of Caenina.

ACTIUM. Scene of battle in which Augustus defeated Antony in 31 B.C.

ADONIS. Young man beloved by Aphrodite and killed by a boar.

ADRASTUS. Leader of the Seven against Thebes and owner of a talking horse.

AEACUS. Judge in the underworld.

AEGIS. Athena's shield.

AEMILIA. Vestal virgin who, accused of letting the fire go out in the temple, relit it by placing her dress on the dead coals. Miraculously, the fabric caught fire and she was vindicated.

AEMILIUS. Early Roman general who defeated Demetrius of Pherae.

AENEAS. Refugee from Troy and legendary ancestor of the Romans.

AESCHYLUS. Founder of Greek drama.

AESON. Father of Jason.

AETHER. Personification of the sky.

AETNA. Sicilian volcano.

AGAMEMNON. Husband of Clytemnestra, who killed him when he returned from Troy.

AJAX. Here, Ajax Oileus, who violated Cassandra.

ALBA LONGA. Ancient city near site where Rome was later founded.

ALBANUS. Lake near town of Alba.

ALCESTIS. Faithful wife who gave up her life for her husband Admetus.

ALCMAEON. Killed his mother Eriphyle and was tormented in hell by the Furies.

ALCMENE. Mother of Hercules by Jupiter.

AMMON. Jupiter Ammon.

AMPHIARAUS. One of the Seven against Thebes, he was swallowed up in a crack in the earth.

AMPHION. Son of Antiope who with his lyre caused rocks to spring up and form the walls of Thebes.

AMYMONE. Daughter of Danaüs who agreed to sleep with Neptune if he would cause a spring to come forth during a drought.

AMYTHAON. Father of Melampus.

ANDROGEUS. Son of Minos killed in a war with Athens and brought back to life by Asclepius, god of medicine.

ANDROMACHE. Hector's wife who, after the fall of Troy, married Helenus.

ANDROMEDA. Daughter of Cassiope, on whose account she was bound to a rock to be eaten by a sea monster. She was rescued by Perseus, who married her.

ANIO. Tributary of the Tiber; the town of Tibur was on its banks beside a waterfall.

ANTAEUS. Lybian giant killed by Hercules.

ANTIGONE. Daughter of Oedipus, betrothed to Haemon.

ANTIMACHUS. Greek poet of Colophon.

ANTINOÜS. Chief suitor of Penelope.

ANTIOPE. Wife of Lycus, who put her away to marry Dirce. Antiope's sons killed Dirce.

ANTONIUS. Mark Antony.

ANUBIS. Egyptian god with head of a dog.

AONIA. Mythic name of Boeotia, where Helicon is situated.

See also HELICON

APELLES. Greek painter of fourth century B.C.

APOLLO. God of the sun and of poetry and music.

APPIAN WAY. Famous road leading south from Rome to Brundisium.

ARAXES. Armenian river.

ARCADIA. Mountainous district of Greece.

ARCHEMORUS. Son of the king of Nemea. The Nemean games originated in the funeral celebrations held after he was killed by a snake.

ARCHYTAS. Mathematician of the fourth century B.C.

ARETHUSA. Wife of Lycotas.

ARGO. Ship of the Greeks who sought the Golden Fleece.

ARGUS. Builder or steersman of the Argo.

ARGUS. Monster with a hundred eyes who was charged with keeping Io after she was changed into a heifer.

ARGYNNUS. Young man who drowned, loved by Agamemnon.

ARIADNE. Daughter of Minos, she was deserted by Theseus after helping him out of the labyrinth. Bacchus fell in love with her and carried her up to heaven.

ARION. Musician saved from the sea by a dolphin.

ARION. Talking horse.

ARRIA. Possibly a kinswoman of Propertius.

ASCANIUS. River in Mysia.

ASCLEPIUS. Greek god of medicine.

ASSISI. Probably Propertius' birthplace.

ATALANTA. Young woman famous for her prowess in the footrace. See also MILANION

ATHAMANIA. A district of ancient Epirus in present-day Albania.

ATLAS. Mauretanian king changed into a mountain on which heaven rested.

ATTICA. The province of Athens.

AUGUSTUS. Surname of Octavian after he became emperor, and of subsequent Roman emperors.

AURORA. Goddess of dawn.

AVERNUS. Lake near Naples said to be the gate of hell, and hence hell itself.

BACTRA. Ancient capital of Bactria, in Persia.

BAIAE. Resort on the Bay of Naples.

BASSUS. Friend of Propertius.

BISTONIA. Thrace.

BOÖTES. Northern constellation.

BOREAS. God of the north wind.

BRENNUS. Leader of Gallic horde that attacked Delphi in 279 B.C.

BRIMO. Proserpine.

BRISEIS. Daughter of Brises and prize of Achilles, from whom she was taken by Agamemnon.

BRUTUS. Early Roman leader who saved the city from kingship.

CACUS. Monster killed by Hercules for stealing cattle.

CADMUS. Founder of Boeotian Thebes.

CAENINA. Town in Latium.

CALAIS. Son of the north wind.

CALCHAS. Prophet who told the Greeks to sacrifice Iphigenia.

CALLIMACHUS. Alexandrian poet, born in Cyrene, greatly admired by Propertius.

CALLIOPE. Muse of epic and other poetry and greatest of the Muses.

CALLISTO. Nymph changed into the constellation Ursa Major.

CALVUS. Poet and friend of Catullus. See also QUINTILIA

CALYPSO. Goddess abandoned by Odysseus.

CAMILLUS. Roman general of an early period.

CAMPANIA. Fertile province in Italy.

CAMPUS. Campus Martius, a place of assembly, games, military drills, and so on, in Rome.

CANNAE. Site of a battle in which Hannibal defeated the Romans.

CAPANEUS. One of the Seven against Thebes, he was blighted by a thunderbolt for offending Zeus.

CAPENE GATE. City gate on the Appian Way.

CARPATHIAN. Part of the Mediterranean named the Carpathian Sea after the island Carpathus.

CASSIOPE. Greek port on the Ionian Sea.

CASTOR. See POLLUX

CATULLUS. Famous Roman poet.

CAŸSTER. River in Lydia which flows into the Aegean Sea near Ephesus.

CERAUNIA. Dangerous promontory near Epirus.

CERBERUS. Three-headed dog guarding entrance to hell.

CHARON. Ferryman of the underworld.

CHARYBDIS. Whirlpool between Italy and Sicily, personified as a female monster.

CHIRON. Centaur renowned for his knowledge of medicine.

CIRCE. Famous witch.

CITHAERON. Mountain in Greece sacred to Bacchus and the Muses.

CLAUDIA. Claudia Quinta, whose rescue of the statue of Cybele when the ship carrying it struck a sandbar cleared her of an accusation of unchastity.

CLAUDIUS. Conqueror of Syracuse in Second Punic War and ancestor of Marcellus.

CLITUMNUS. Small Umbrian river.

CLYTEMNESTRA. Wife and murderess of Agamemnon.

CONON. Greek astronomer.

CORA. Town in Latium.

CORINNA. Famous Greek poetess contemporary with Pindar.

CORNELIA. Daughter of Scribonia and Cornelius Scipio and wife of L. Aemilius Paullus, consul in 34 B.C. and censor in 22 B.C.

COS. Island off coast of Caria famous for its wine and cloth and as birthplace of the poet Philetas.

COSSUS. Early consul.

CRASSUS. General who lost his life, as did also his son, in the disaster at Carrhae in 53 B.C.

CREÜSA. Jason's wife, burned to death by a fiery robe which Medea sent her.

CROESUS. Lydian king renowned for his wealth.

CUMAE, SIBYL OF. Prophetess of the town of Cumae, renowned for her great age.

CURES. Ancient capital of the Sabines.

CURII, CURIATII. Three brothers from Alba who were slain by the Horatii, three brothers of Rome.

CURTIUS. Roman hero who rode his horse into a giant crack in the Forum to stop the earthquake that had opened up the chasm.

CYBELE. Phrygian goddess widely worshiped in Rome.

CYRENE. Birthplace of Callimachus.

CYTHEREAN. Sacred to Venus.

CYZICUS. Town on the Propontis.

DAHAN. Region east of the Caspian Sea.

DANAË. Mother of Perseus by Zeus, who impregnated her by coming to her as a shower of gold while she was locked up in a tower.

DANAÏAN. Greek.

DANAÏDES. The fifty daughters of Danaüs, each of whom, except Hypermnestra, murdered her husband. For this crime they were condemned to pour water perpetually into a broken cistern in hell.

DAPHNIS. Shepherd in Vergil's pastorals.

DECII. Three generals—father, son, and grandson—who were all patriotic martyrs.

DEIDAMIA. Achilles' girlfriend and mother by him of Pyrrhus.

DEMOPHOÖN. (1) Son of Theseus. (2) Friend of Propertius. See also PHYLLIS

DEMOSTHENES. Famous Greek orator.

DEUCALION. He and his wife were the only survivors of the legendary Greek flood.

DIANA. Italian goddess of the moon, virginity, childbirth, hunting, and magic, identified with the Greek Artemis.

DIONE. Here, Aphrodite.

DIRCE. Killed for unjustly persecuting Antiope. See also ANTIOPE; LYCUS.

DODONA. City in Epirus in northern Greece, site of a famous oracle of Zeus.

DORIS. Daughter of Oceanus who was the mother of 100 (sometimes 50) sea nymphs.

DOROZANTUM. Probably a corruption of a place-name.

ELECTRA. Sister of Orestes.

ELIS. Region in Greece famous for horse racing, where Olympic games were held.

ENDYMION. Beautiful youth who offended Zeus and was condemned to eternal sleep; beloved by Luna.

ENIPEUS. River and river-god of Thessaly, whose form Poseidon assumed in order to seduce Tyro.

ENNIUS. First great Roman poet.

EPICURUS. Greek philosopher.

EREBUS. God of darkness and, by extension, Hades.

ERINNA. Famous Greek poetess of Lesbos.

ERIPHYLE. Wife of Amphiaraus who, in return for a golden necklace from Polynices, persuaded her husband to join the Seven against Thebes.

ERYTHEA. Legendary western island where the Geryones lived.

ESQUILINE. One of the hills of Rome, on which Propertius lived.

EUBOEA. Island in the Aegean Sea.

EUMENIDES. "The gracious ones," a euphemism for the Furies.

EUROPA. Sister of Cadmus, and mother of Sarpedon and Minos by Jupiter, who came to her in the form of a bull.

EVADNE. Wife of Capaneus who threw herself into her husband's funeral fire.

EVANDER. Arcadian exile who settled where Rome was later built.

FABIUS. Roman general famous for his delaying tactics in Second Punic War.

FALERNIAN. Wine from the district of Falernus.

FERETRIAN JUPITER. Jupiter Feretrius, one of Jupiter's designations.

FORUM. Open place in Rome where affairs of state were conducted.

GALAESUS. River in lower Italy.

GALATEA. Sea nymph loved by Polyphemus.

GALLA. Aelia Galla, wife of Postumus.

GALLUS. (1) Friend of Propertius mentioned in I.5, I.10, I.13, and I.20. (2) Rome's first great elegiac poet, who celebrated his mistress Lycoris. (3) Son of Arria and perhaps related to Propertius; perhaps also the soldier mentioned in I.21.

GERYON. Spanish monster with three bodies whose oxen were stolen by Hercules.

GETAE. Scythian tribe.

GLAUCUS. Greek fisherman who was changed into a sea-god.

GORGON. Any one of the three daughters of Phorcus, but especially Medusa; the sight of a Gorgon turned the beholder to stone.

GYGAEUS. Lake near Sardis in Lydia.

HAEMON. Son of Creon who killed himself when Antigone died.

HAEMONIA. Old name of Thessaly; Achilles' horses were Haemonian.

HANNIBAL. Famous Carthaginian general.

HECATE. Goddess of crossroads and of enchantments, identified with Diana, Luna, and Proserpine.

HECTOR. Greatest of the Trojan warriors.

HELICON. Mountain sacred to the Muses and to Apollo.

HELLE. Daughter of Athamas who, escaping on the back of a winged golden ram, fell into the sea—named the Hellespont after her—and drowned.

HERA. Juno, Jupiter's wife.

HERCULES. Legendary Greek hero.

HERMIONE. Daughter of Helen and Menelaus.

HESIOD. Greek poet born at Ascra.

HESPERIDES. Nymphs who watched a garden of golden apples on a legendary island beyond Mount Atlas.

HESPERUS. The evening star.

HIPPOCRENE. Fountain on Helicon sprung from a blow of Pegasus' hoof.

HIPPODAMIA. Young woman won by Pelops after he defeated her father in a chariot race.

HIPPOLYTUS. Son of Theseus and Hippolyte. See also PHAEDRA

HORATII. See CURII.

HORATIO. Horatius Cocles, who defended a bridge single-handed against an Etruscan army.

HOROS. An astrologer.

HYLAEUS. Centaur who attacked Atalanta and wounded Milanion, who defended her.

HYLAS. Hercules' catamite.

HYMENAEUS. God of marriage.

HYPERMNESTRA. The only one of Danaüs' fifty daughters who did not kill her husband.

ICARIUS. Killed by peasants to whom he had given wine, he became the star Arcturus in the constellation Boötes.

IDA. Famous mountain where Paris judged the beauty contest in which Aphrodite, Hera, and Athena participated.

IDALIA. Mountain in Cyprus sacred to Aphrodite.

IDAS. Strove with Apollo for the love of Marpessa.

ILION, ILIUM. Troy.

ILLYRIA. Roman province on the Adriatic.

INO. Daughter of Cadmus who, caused to go mad by Hera, leapt into the sea and was changed into the sea-goddess Leucothoë.

IO. Loved by Zeus. Changed by Hera into a cow, she later became the goddess Isis.

IOPE. Either the wife of Theseus or the mother of Andromeda.

IPHIGENIA. Daughter of Agamemnon sacrificed in expiation for a crime committed by her father. In some accounts Diana saves her at the last moment by putting a deer on the altar in her stead.

IRUS. Beggar at Odysseus' palace.

ISMARA. City and mountain in southern Thrace.

ITYS. Son of Tereus and Procne, killed by his mother and served to his father as food in revenge for Tereus' rape and maiming of Procne's sister, Philomela.

IXION. Strapped to an eternally revolving wheel in hell for attempting to seduce Juno.

JANUS. God of doorways, represented with two faces.

JASON. Hero of the quest for the Golden Fleece.

JUGURTHA. Numidian king conquered by Marius.

JULIA. Augustus' daughter and Cornelia's half sister.

JULUS. Son of Aeneas, also called Ascanius.

LAIS. Name of two beautiful Corinthian prostitutes.

LALAGE. One of Cynthia's slaves.

LANUVIUM. Town near Rome.

LATRIS. One of Cynthia's slaves.

LAVINIUM. City Aeneas founded and named for his wife, Lavinia.

LECHAEUM. Western port of Corinth.

LEDA. Mother of Helen.

LEMNIAN QUEEN. Hypsipyle, abandoned by Jason.

LEPIDUS. One of Cornelia's sons.

LESBIA. Clodia, mistress of Catullus.

LETHE. River in hell whose waters brought forgetfulness to those who drank.

LEUCADIA. See VARRO

LEUCOTHOË. A sea-goddess, the deification of Ino.

LIBER. Bacchus.

LINUS. Taught the lyre to Orpheus and Hercules, the latter of whom killed him with a blow of the lyre.

LUCIFER. The morning star.

LUCINA. Juno Lucina, goddess of childbirth.

LUCUMO. Leader of one of the three tribes of Rome after the Sabine war.

LUPERCALIA. Ancient Roman festival held by the Luperci; possibly connected with Lupercus, who was sometimes identified with Faunus, a rural deity.

LUPERCUS. Here, a son of Arria.

LYCINNA. Initiated Propertius in the sexual arts.

LYCOTAS. Pseudonym for an acquaintance of Propertius, perhaps identical with Postumus.

LYCURGUS. Thracian king who, driven mad for opposing and jailing Dionysus, killed his own son.

LYCUS. King of Thebes who put away Antiope and married Dirce.

LYDIA. Region in Asia Minor.

LYGDAMUS. One of Cynthia's slaves.

LYNCEUS. Poet and friend of Propertius.

MACHAON. Greek physician.

MAEANDER. Winding river in Asia Minor.

MAECENAS. Friend of Augustus and patron of Vergil, Horace, and Propertius.

MAENADS. Bacchantes.

MAMURIUS. Legendary bronzeworker.

MARCELLUS. Nephew of Octavian who died at Baiae in 23 B.C.

MARCIAN AQUEDUCT. Aqueduct named after Quintus Marcius Rex.

MARIUS. Famous Roman general who defeated Jugurtha.

MARO. Here, a statue of the companion of Bacchus.

MAUSOLUS. King of Caria whose tomb, built for him by his widow at Halicarnassus, is one of the Seven Wonders of the World.

MEDEA. An enchantress who, betrayed by her lover Jason, whom she had helped to bring back the Golden Fleece, killed her children by Jason and caused his new bride to be burned to death.

MEDES. Inhabitants of ancient Media, bounded by Armenia, Assyria, and Parthia.

MELAMPUS. Famous physician and fortune-teller who tried unsuccessfully to steal the cattle of Iphiclus so that his brother Bias might marry Pero. Here Melampus himself may be the suitor.

MEMNON. Aurora's son, said to be black, killed by Achilles at Troy.

MENANDER. Greek comic playwright.

MENELAUS. Helen's husband.

METHYMNA. Town on island of Lesbos.

MEVANIA. Umbrian town.

MILANION. Successful wooer of Atalanta.

MIMNERMUS. Early Greek elegiac poet.

MINOS. King of Crete, later a judge in hell.

MINOTAUR. Monster born of Pasiphaë and a bull.

MISENUS. Aeneas' trumpet player, buried near Baiae.

MITHRIDATES. King of Pontus who committed suicide after being defeated by Pompey.

MUTINA. Site of a battle between Antony and Octavian.

MYRON. Athenian sculptor.

MYRRHA. Maiden who fell in love with her father and was transformed into a myrrh tree.

MYSIA. Region in Asia Minor, on the Hellespont and the Aegean Sea.

NAIADS. Water nymphs.

NAUPLIUS. To avenge the death of his son Palamedes, killed by the Greeks, he burned signal fires on a dangerous headland, thus shipwrecking the Greeks as they returned from Troy.

NAXOS. Island in the Aegean Sea famous for its wines.

NEMI. Lake in the Alban Hills.

NEREIDES. Sea nymphs, daughters of Doris and Nereus.

NESTOR. Greek king who was the oldest and wisest of the Greek heroes before Troy.

NEURI. Scythian tribe.

NEW FIELD GARDENS. Gardens built by Maecenas on the site of an old cemetery on the Esquiline.

NILE GODDESS. Isis.

NIOBE. For boasting that her children were more beautiful than Apollo and Artemis she was turned to stone and the children were killed.

NIREUS. Next to Achilles, most beautiful of the Greek heroes at siege of Troy.

NOMAS. One of Cynthia's slaves.

NOMENTUM. Town near Rome.

OCNUS. Figure in hell represented as eternally braiding a straw rope whose other end was being eaten by an ass.

OETA. Mountain between Thessaly and Aetolia, where Hercules died. He was taken from there to heaven and married Hebe.

OMPHALE. Lydian queen admired and served by Hercules disguised as a woman.

OREITHYIA. Daughter of Erechtheus who was carried off by Boreas.

ORICOS. Port in Greek Illyria.

ORONTES. River near Antioch.

OROPS. An astrologer.

ORPHEUS. Famous lyre player, husband of Eurydice.

ORTYGIA. Island of Delos.

PACTOLUS. River in Lydia famed for its gold-bearing sands.

PAETUS. Friend of Propertius who drowned at sea.

PAGASA. Thessalian port where the Argo was built.

PALATINE. One of the seven hills of Rome.

PANTHUS. One of Cynthia's slaves.

PARCAE. The Fates.

PARILIA. The festival of Pales on April 21.

PARIS. Priam's son who chose Aphrodite as the most beautiful of goddesses in a contest on Mount Ida and in exchange was enabled to carry off Helen, Menelaus' wife. This act started the Trojan War.

PARNASSUS. Mountain sacred to the Muses and to Apollo. Delphi and the Castalian spring were at its foot. The Gauls were driven from Delphi by storm and earthquake in 279 B.C.

PARTHENIE. Cynthia's nurse.

PARTHENIUS. Mountain in Arcadia.

PARTHIANS. Scythian nomads found north of the Caspian.

PASIPHAË. Seduced a bull by putting on wooden horns and thus became mother of the Minotaur.

PATROCLUS. Friend of Achilles, killed by Hector.

PAULLUS. L. Aemilius Paullus. See CORNELIA

PEGASUS. Winged horse sprung from the blood of Medusa.

PEGE. Mysian fountain.

PELEUS. Achilles' father.

PENELOPE. Wife of Odysseus.

PENTHEUS. King of Thebes who was discovered spying on the ceremonies of bacchantes, led by his mother, and was torn to bits by them.

PERGAMA. The citadel of Troy.

PERILLUS. Bronzeworker who made a hollow bull for the tyrant Phalaris, in which criminals were to be roasted alive. The sculptor was reputedly the first victim.

PERIMEDE. Legendary sorceress.

PERSEPHONE. Queen of hell, wife of Dis.

PERSES. Macedonian king who claimed descent from Achilles and Hercules; defeated by Cornelia's ancestor in 168 B.C.

PERSEUS. Greek hero who received winged shoes from Mercury, killed Medusa, and rescued and married Andromeda. Their son Perses was progenitor of the Persians.

PERUSIA. Town in Etruria besieged by Octavian.

PETALE. One of Cynthia's slaves.

PHAEDRA. Sister of Ariadne who fell in love with her son-in-law Hippolytus and killed herself. Propertius' story that she tried to poison Hippolytus is otherwise unknown.

PHAROS. Lighthouse near Alexandria.

PHASIS. River in Colchis emptying into the Black Sea.

PHILETAS. Famous Alexandrian poet from the island of Cos.

PHILIPPI. City in Macedonia where Octavian and Antony defeated Brutus and Cassius.

PHILOCTETES. Bitten by a snake on the way to Troy and abandoned because of the stench of the wound, but later retrieved and cured because an oracle told the Greeks they needed his bow (or arrows) to win. He later killed Paris.

PHINEUS. Thracian king blinded and tormented by the Harpies for having his sons blinded. In hell his food was defiled so as to be inedible.

PHOEBE. See POLLUX

PHOENIX. Companion of Achilles who was healed of blindness by Chiron.

PHRYNE. Athenian prostitute so rich she offered to rebuild Thebes.

PHYLLIS. (1) Daughter of Sithon of Thrace who, deserted by Demophoön, killed herself and was changed into an almond tree. (2) Mistress of Propertius' friend styled "Demophoön." (3) In IV.8, a prostitute.

PINDUS. Mountain in Thrace.

PIRAEUS. Port of Athens, about 5 miles away and connected by long walls.

PLEIADES. Seven daughters of Atlas and Pleione who were placed in the heavens as a constellation.

POLLUX. Son of Tyndareus and Leda, brother of Castor and Helen. Castor and Pollux carried off Hilaira and Phoebe.

POLYDORUS. Son of Priam who was killed by Polymnestor, his guardian, for his gold.

POLYPHEMUS. Cyclops blinded by Odysseus. Loved Galatea.

POMPEY. Famous Roman general and triumvir.

PONTICUS. Poet and acquaintance of Propertius.

POSTUMUS. Perhaps a pseudonym for Lycotas, friend of Propertius.

PRAENESTE. Town east of Rome, famous for its oracle; now Palestrina.

PRIAM. King of Troy.

PROMETHEUS. Created the human race out of clay and brought fire from heaven, for which he was punished by being tied to a mountain where vultures gnawed at his entrails.

PROPONTIS. Sea of Marmora, between the Hellespont and the Bosporus.

PROTESILAUS. First Greek killed at Troy, he was allowed to leave hell to visit his bride.

PTOLEMY. Name of a line of Egyptian rulers.

PYRRHUS. King of Epirus who invaded Italy in third century B.C.

PYTHON. Huge snake killed at Delphi by Apollo.

QUINTILIA. Mistress of Calvus.

REMUS. Brother of Romulus.

ROMULUS. Founder of Rome.

SATURN. The reign of Saturn was considered a golden age in Italy.

SCAEAN GATE. Gate of Troy where Achilles was killed.

SCIPIO. One of two Roman generals of the same name who conquered the Carthaginians.

SCIRON. Legendary robber on the cliff road between Corinth and Athens.

SCRIBONIA. Mother of Cornelia and later wife of Augustus.

SCYLLA. (1) Rock on Italian coast, opposite Charybdis, personified as a sea monster. (2) Daughter and betrayer of Nisus. Propertius confuses the two in IV.4.

SCYTHIA. Region north and east of the Black Sea inhabited by nomadic tribes.

SEMELE. Mother of Bacchus.

SEMIRAMIS. Babylonian queen.

SIBYL. Any of several female fortune-tellers and oracles, the most important of whom was the prophetess at Cumae.

SIDON. Phoenician city.

SILENUS. Lewd attendant of Bacchus.

SISYPHUS. Condemned in hell to push a huge boulder up a hill, which always rolled down when near the top.

STYX. River in hell.

SYCAMBRI. Teutonic people who defeated the Romans in Gaul in 16 B.C.

SYPHAX. Libyan king defeated and captured by Scipio in Second Punic War.

SYRTES. Two inlets on Mediterranean coast of northern Africa with dangerous sandbars.

TANTALUS. In Hades, tormented by hunger and thirst while fruit and water were close by but beyond his reach.

TARPEIA. Maiden who opened the city of Rome to the Sabines for "what they wore on their arms"; instead of giving her their bracelets, as she expected, they killed her by throwing their shields on her.

TARPEIAN HILL. A rock on the Capitoline, a hill sacred to Jupiter.

TARQUIN. Roman king.

TATIUS. Sabine king who fought Romulus and became coruler of Rome.

TAYGETUS. Mountain range in Sparta.

TEIA. Prostitute.

TELEGONUS. Son of Odysseus and Circe who founded Tusculum and Praeneste.

TELEPHUS. Wounded by Achilles' spear but cured by its rust.

TELLUS. Earth.

THAIS. Famous Athenian prostitute.

THAMYRAS. Thracian poet stricken blind for challenging the Muses to a contest of song.

THEBES. (1) Greek city founded by Cadmus. (2) In IV.5, Egyptian city.

THERMODON. River in Asia Minor, on whose banks lived the Amazons.

THESEUS. King of Athens who abandoned Ariadne after she helped him out of the labyrinth.

THETIS. Sea-goddess and mother of Achilles.

TIBUR. Town on the falls of the Anio, now Tivoli.

TIRESIAS. Theban who was blinded because he saw Pallas naked; later given the power of prophecy.

TISIPHONE. One of the Furies.

TITHONUS. Consort of Aurora, who gave him immortality but neglected to protect him against old age.

TITYOS. Giant punished for attempting to ravish Latona by being stretched out over 9 acres in Hades while vultures fed on his liver.

TOLUMNIUS. King of Veii.

TRITON. Here, a statue of the sea-god Triton.

TULLUS. Friend of Propertius.

TYRE. Chief city of Phoenicia.

TYRO. See ENIPEUS

VARRO. Elegiac poet who celebrated his mistress Leucadia and translated the *Argonautica* of Apollonius Rhodius.

VEII. Town in Etruria.

VELABRUM. Marshy ground beneath the Aventine which was once flooded.

VERGIL. Roman epic poet.

VERTUMNUS. God of change.

VIRDOMARUS. King of the Insubres who was killed fighting the Romans.

XERXES. King of Persia who tried to build a canal across the isthmus of Athos.

ZETES. Son of the north wind.

ZETHUS. Son of Antiope and twin brother of Amphion.